Golden **Flavours** *of* Summer

Golden Flavours *of* Summer

Peter Doyle

Photographs by
Rodney Weidland

Lothian
BOOKS

To Beverley,
my soul mate

PAGE 1: Grilled prawns with tarragon and garlic butter (recipe page 80)

PAGES 2–3: Salad of marron with baby vegetables, herbs and pistou (recipe page 29)

ABOVE: Peter Doyle and his family at their favourite place

ACKNOWLEDGEMENTS

Many thanks to: Barbara Beckett for her encouragement, editing and believing it could happen; Rodney Weidland for his beautiful creative photography; Neville and Joy Hinds for their enduring faith; Paul and Jenny White for the generous use of their amazing house and Jenny's fine cooking; all the staff at Cicada for their help, understanding and good humour; Gail and Pam of Foodservice Equipment International; Michele of Kitchen Kapers; Empire Homewares of Paddington; Tom and Lana, Renee and Dennis, Bianca and Montana for encouragement, ideas and family dinners; all my suppliers at Cicada who have grown accustomed to my strange demands over the years; and last, but not least, the patrons and friends of Cicada—thank you for your support and inspiration over many years.

Cicada, 29 Challis Avenue, Potts Point, Sydney 2011
Celsius°, 66 Pitt Street, Sydney 2000

Thomas C. Lothian Pty Ltd
11 Munro Street, Port Melbourne, Victoria 3207

National Library of Australia
Cataloguing-in-Publication data:

Doyle, Peter John, 1952–.
  Golden flavours of summer.

  Includes index.
  ISBN 0 7344 0147 7.

  1. Cookery. 2. Cookery (Seafood). 3. Desserts. I.
  Weidland, Rodney. II. Title.

641.692

Produced in association with Barbara Beckett Publishing Pty Ltd
14 Hargrave Street, Paddington, Sydney, Australia 2021
Photography by Rodney Weidland
Food by Peter Doyle and styling by Barbara Beckett
Design by Barbara Beckett
Printed in China by Everbest Printing Pty Ltd

Contents

Introduction

I began my cooking career during what I called the iceberg lettuce age. If Australian restaurant cuisine at the time was not quite frozen over, neither had the big thaw started. Thankfully change was shortly to arrive in the guise of the nouvelle cuisine movement—the beginning of a modern Australian cuisine.

The modern world of food owes a great debt to a few chefs working in France in the 1970s—Michel Guerard, the Troisgros Brothers, Roger Vergé, Georges Blanc, Alain Chapel and a few others formed the Bande de Bocuse. These chefs craved flexibility and room for experimentation—their curiosities had been denied by Haute Cuisine rules and regulations which had not changed for nearly fifty years.

Food was suddenly news, not just for the select few, but for anyone interested in good food. Paul Bocuse was presented with the Légion d'Honneur for 'services to the promotion of French cuisine to the world' in 1975 at the Lunch of the Century. The historical menu featured revolutionary concepts, ideas and techniques with food. The salmon on the menu was finely sliced, cooked quickly in a teflon frying pan and the sauce was poured under instead of over, the fish. Some of the basic guidelines of nouvelle cuisine such as shorter menus, natural flavours, lighter sauces, regular shopping at the markets, diet and health, invention and innovation, form the basis of great cuisine throughout the world today.

Although there was some confusion, and some very unhappy marriages of ingredients (Poached snapper with kiwi fruit and strawberry sauce), this was understandable in a new movement. But if you browse through any large supermarket today the effects of this movement are evident in every aisle. Good food stimulates and surprises. It's better to choose between fifteen varieties of salad leaves than being faced with the dilemma of taking home the iceberg variety everyday.

My curiosity led Beverley, our daughter Renee and me to France in 1978. For eight months we travelled through the provinces of France in our campervan, soaking up a very different and stimulating way of life. We visited great vineyards, cafes, restaurants, markets as well as the best surf breaks. I would call into the finest restaurants where nouvelle cuisine was cooked and ask if I could work in the kitchen for a week. I enjoyed working

RIGHT: My grand-daughter, Montana, with our favourite barbecue dish Grilled prawns with tarragon and garlic butter (recipe page 80)

with Roger Vergé, Georges Blanc, Pierre and Jean Troisgros, for which I'm forever grateful. We dined at Michel Guerard's, Alain Chapel's, and at Paul Bocuse's restaurant, and many others. We consumed the local cheeses and specialties at all the markets. It was a very exciting time and helped form my philosophy of food. It showed me that the best food experiences were not elaborate or fussy, even at the great restaurants. Good food was based on traditional flavour combinations of the finest ingredients and sound techniques. For instance at Guerard's the puff pastry was the lightest, yet still the most buttery, the crayfish between the pastry was perfectly cooked and the sauce light, yet full of flavour and heightened by the freshest of herbs. Good food was simple food at heart. Flavours were always enhanced, not dominated. It formed my mantra: 'I like the interplay of classic harmonious flavours enhancing the main ingredient. Restraint and simplicity are important qualities for a perfectly cooked dish.'

Golden flavours of summer is a collection of recipes based on seasonal produce available during the warmer parts of the year. Throughout the chapter introductions and recipes I talk about shopping for quality summer ingredients. I've mostly concentrated on easy to acquire produce. Some of this produce may only be available at the quality purveyors in your local area. But

shopping is half the fun of cooking and most of the time a great source of inspiration. If you see something different, buy it and accept the challenge.

Other qualities very useful when cooking are planning and common sense. Even the recipes for quickly cooked dishes will benefit from planning. Take the time to read the recipe thoroughly, check the ingredients list and break down the preparation into small stages. It will make cooking seem less daunting and build your confidence. It's just as important to plan an achievable menu in terms of a balanced work load as it is of balanced dishes. Remember, you want to enjoy the company of your family or invited friends over a few glasses of wine, but you will miss out on all the fun if you spend all night behind the stove. If you have planned a complex main course, start and finish with easily prepared recipes.

At Cicada we have at our disposal all the equipment necesary in a professional kitchen. The domestic kitchen does not need to be stocked with an expensive array of equipment but a few essentials will inspire better cooking. The list of items that follows may seem long but there is no need to acquire everything at once. I would recommend that you buy the best quality heavy-bottomed range of saucepans you can afford. Good knives and a large stockpot (16–20 litres) are also a good investment and will last a lifetime. Other useful equipment, apart from a blender, food processor and an electric mixer, include a mandoline for fine slicing; an instant thermometer for inserting into hot food; deep-frying thermometer; silicon-coated non-stick baking sheets; heavy flat trays; fine strainer and conical sieve; pasta machine; balloon-whisk for eggwhites; a couple of good timers and a set of kitchen scales.

Ultimately good cooking is more about what you feel like cooking and eating. Respect and care for food shows in the quality of your cooking. If you love food and enjoy yourself whilst cooking you will create good food. This book is full of recipes for dishes that I like to eat. I hope you will be stimulated to cook them and even better, to use them as guidelines for your inspirations. Please feel free to experiment—take part of my recipes and with a quick referral to the philosophy mentioned above, have fun creating your own recipes.

If you ask a winemaker how to learn about wine, they will tell you to taste as many wines as possible, and then taste some more. Food is no different. Pay attention to what well-prepared food tastes like, what you enjoy and what you don't like. Build up a memory taste bank and you will develop an understanding of why this ingredient complements that taste. Then you will have created a springboard to develop your own recipes.

Bon appetit!

PETER DOYLE, SYDNEY

MEASUREMENTS

1 teaspoon	*= 5 ml*	*2/3 cup*	*= 166 ml*
1 tablespoon	*= 20 ml*	*3/4 cup*	*= 175 ml*
1/5 cup	*= 50 ml*	*4/5 cup*	*= 200 ml*
1/4 cup	*= 62.5 ml*	*1 cup*	*= 250 ml*
1/3 cup	*= 83 ml*		
2/5 cup	*= 100 ml*		
1/2 cup	*= 125 ml*		
3/5 cup	*= 150 ml*		

All eggs are 60 g
Butter is unsalted
Sugar is caster sugar unless stated otherwise

At the beach

Starters and snacks

Starters and snacks, tapas, antipasto, meze—all these words conjure up an anticipation of delicious bites. They have an ease and freshness that evokes food eaten at a leisurely pace in a relaxing atmosphere. The bites could range from a celery stick dipped in Anchoiade to a Croûton spread with Samfaina. They could be individual first course dishes but as most of them have complementary flavours it's fun to serve a few together at a picnic or buffet. Try Hummus, Tarator and Dukkah, or Samfaina and Romesco, or Tapenade and Anchoiade. All are packed with flavour from the first taste to the last. They give you a chance to graze through different flavour spectrums while stimulating your appetite for more. Serve them with delicious breads and salad vegetables.

The Herb ricotta with artichokes, Buffalo milk mozzarella with ox-heart tomatoes and the Mussels and oysters are other examples of shared picnic dishes. They encourage guests to relax, take their time and enjoy the moment.

The Tomato consommé is the essence of summer and very adaptable. Serve it chilled and garnished simply with basil and diced tomato as a starter, or heated for dinner.

The Tuna tartare with wasabi tobiko and spice-crusted tuna on soba and cucumber noodles and the Fennel-cured salmon are more substantial starters that capture the mood of summer. The flavours of sesame oil, soy, ginger, chilli, and lime deliciously enhance the taste of raw or lightly sealed tuna and combine to really awaken your tastebuds.

Simplicity and flexibility are the essence of this chapter. Most of the recipes have been created so they can be easily transported for picnics and outdoor eating. They are also suitable for special occasions. Many of the dishes are served at room temperature or chilled to highlight their special flavours. Think of these dishes as light tastes to be enjoyed in a relaxing summery way.

RIGHT: Herb ricotta with artichokes, radish and olive salad (recipe overleaf)

Herb ricotta with artichokes,
radish and olive salad

A perfect beach snack or part of a picnic. Serve with a bottle of chilled white wine and let everyone help themselves.

Ingredients

1½ cups fresh ricotta cheese, drained

2 tablespoons chopped fresh flat-leaf parsley

1 tablespoon roughly chopped fresh chervil

4 tablespoons Lemon vinaigrette (page 129)

1½ green shallots, chopped

Sea salt and freshly ground black pepper

3 tablespoons olive oil

Few fresh chervil sprigs

8–12 artichokes, marinated, drained

6 tablespoons small black olives

3 tablespoons broad beans, podded, blanched, shelled

12 oven-dried tomatoes or fresh, sliced tomatoes

12 red radishes, halved

Extra fresh chervil sprigs

8–16 slices crostini or olive bread, toasted

Serves 8

To make the herb ricotta, place the ricotta in a bowl and mix in the parsley, chervil, lemon vinaigrette, and shallots, then season with salt and pepper. Cover and refrigerate if not using immediately.

To serve, spoon the herb ricotta onto the centre of a platter or individual plates and sprinkle with black pepper, olive oil and a few chervil sprigs. Place the artichokes, olives, broad beans, oven-dried tomatoes and radishes colourfully around the ricotta and garnish with the extra chervil sprigs. Serve with the olive bread or crostini.

Fresh figs
with mascarpone and gorgonzola

Figs have to be perfectly ripe, sweet and softened to display their full glory. In this appetiser the mascarpone tames the gorgonzola a little, both blending deliciously with the sweetness of the figs and bitterness of the salad.

Ingredients

100 g gorgonzola, crumbled

100 g mascarpone

1½ tablespoons olive oil + extra

Freshly ground black pepper

1 cup red radicchio, leaves torn

1 cup curly endive, white part only

10 ripe figs

½ cup extra-virgin olive oil

1 tablespoon balsamic vinegar + extra

10 Crostini (page 134), if preferred

Serves 10

To prepare the cheese, place the gorgonzola and mascarpone in a bowl and mix together with a wooden spoon. Pour 1½ tablespoons of olive oil over the cheese mixture, add a grinding of black pepper and mix into the cheese. The cheese doesn't have to be perfectly blended and actually is best with a slightly crumbled texture.

To serve, toss the radicchio and curly endive in a bowl with a little olive oil and balsamic vinegar. Carefully place a small portion of the salad in the centre of each serving plate. Trim the stem of each fig and cut in half lengthwise. Place a small mound of the cheese mixture on top of each fig half and grind a little pepper over the cheese. Place 2 fig halves on each plate over the salad leaves. Drizzle with extra balsamic vinegar and olive oil, and serve with crostini or crusty bread to mop up the juices.

Anchoiade

A small bowl of anchoiade will stimulate the palate and appetite—an ideal beginning to any picnic. Pack other dips such as Tapenade, Dukkah, Hummus, Tarator, Samfaina or Romesco. Take some crusty bread and some vegetables to dip—radishes, capsicums, cucumbers, celery and fennel.

Ingredients

110 g anchovy fillets, rinsed

1 garlic clove, minced

4 black olives, pitted

2 teaspoons white-wine vinegar

1 cup extra-virgin olive oil

Freshly ground black pepper

Serves 10

To prepare the anchoiade, place the anchovies, garlic, olives and vinegar in the bowl of a food processor and purée while you pour the olive oil through the top in a steady stream until the purée is smooth. Transfer to a small bowl or an airtight container. Keep the anchoiade refrigerated, but return to room temperature before serving (you may need to add a little water depending on the thickness of the anchoiade).

Clear tomato soup
with basil

A clear soup with a subtle but haunting depth of flavour. The perfect time to make this simple soup is when ripe tomatoes are in abundance at the height of summer. Once you find out how easy it is you will make it often—try varying the garnish each time.

Ingredients

Soup

3 kg ripe egg-shaped (roma) tomatoes

2 celery stalks, chopped finely

1 carrot, peeled, sliced finely

1 onion, peeled, sliced

1 red serrano or similiar hot chilli, seeded, quartered

1 bayleaf

Sea salt and freshly ground black pepper

1 ripe egg-shaped tomato (roma), seeded, diced

1 green shallot, cleaned, finely sliced

Small fresh basil leaves

Tapenade crostini (page 134) or fresh crusty bread

Serves 10

To make the soup, cut the tomatoes in half and slice crosswise into several slices. Place the tomatoes and any juices into a heavy-bottomed stainless steel saucepan and add the celery, carrot, onion, chilli and bay leaf. Bring the contents to the boil over a medium heat. Reduce the heat and simmer for 15 minutes without disturbing except to stir gently once or twice. Remove the saucepan from the heat and allow the soup to settle for a few minutes. Carefully ladle the soup through a very fine strainer lined with muslin. Season to taste with salt and pepper. This soup can be served hot or chilled.

To serve, garnish the soup bowls with the diced tomato, green shallot and basil leaves before serving. Serve with tapenade crostini or fresh crusty bread on the side.

LEFT: Clear tomato soup with basil

RIGHT: Fennel-cured salmon with shaved cucumber and dill salad (recipe overleaf)

Fennel-cured salmon
with shaved cucumber and dill salad

A perfect picnic starter or lunch entrée, light and full of refreshing flavours.

Ingredients

2 cups sea salt

2½ tablespoons black peppercorns, coarsely ground

1¾ cups sugar

3 tablespoons fennel seeds

750–g side of salmon, skinned, pin bones removed

1 cucumber, peeled, cut in 5 cm lengths

2½ tablespoons Lemon vinaigrette (page 129)

Freshly ground black pepper

3 red radishes

3 tablespoons fresh dill fronds

Serves 8

To prepare the salmon, mix the salt, pepper, sugar and fennel seeds. Remove the pin bones in the salmon by feeling for them with your finger tips down the length of the fillet near the centre from the head end down. Using tweezers or long-nosed pliers remove any remaining bones by pulling in a firm, but gentle, motion up and towards the head of the fillet. Take a non-reactive container long enough to hold the salmon and sprinkle one-third of the seasoning mixture on to the bottom of the tray. Place the salmon on top and cover with the remaining mixture. Cover with cling-wrap and refrigerate for 12–24 hours.

Remove the salmon from the marinade and wash it well in plenty of water. Dry thoroughly and leave aside. Slice the salmon, as you would for smoked salmon into thin slices on an angle, and arrange a few slices on chilled plates, weaving them to give them a little height and form.

To prepare the cucumber, finely shave the cucumber down one side on a mandoline slicer or a vegetable peeler until you reach the seeds, turn onto another side and continue shaving and repeat around the seed core. Discard the seed core. Toss the cucumber with some lemon vinaigrette in a small bowl and season with black pepper.

To serve, arrange the shaved cucumber over the salmon on each plate. Cut the radish into very fine rounds on the mandoline or with a sharp knife, and remove the slices to a cutting board. Julienne the radish very finely with a sharp knife and sprinkle over the cucumber. Sprinkle on the dill fronds and drizzle a little lemon vinaigrette around the salmon. Serve with slices of ciabatta or crusty bread.

SALMON CARPACCIO
Finely sliced raw salmon served as a carpaccio could be used instead of the cured salmon in this salad. Follow the recipe above allowing for more lemon vinaigrette to help marinate the raw salmon. Very finely shaved fennel could also replace the cucumber in early summer for added texture and a stronger flavour.

Pan bagnat

Great picnic food—a pan bagnat is the Provençal version of a sophisticated salad roll. Hollow out the crisp rolls and fill with your choice of Niçoise flavours.

Ingredients

4 crisp bread rolls

2 ripe egg-shaped (roma) tomatoes, seeded, sliced

2 Roasted red capsicums (page 137)

16 black olives, pitted

2 spring onions, sliced finely

Sea salt and freshly ground black pepper

2 tablespoons Red-wine vinaigrette (page 129)

6 artichoke hearts, marinated in oil

2 hard-boiled eggs, sliced

7 good quality anchovy fillets

2 tablespoons Pistou (page 29)

Serves 4

To prepare the pan bagnat, slice the top off each bread roll and remove most of the soft centre, being careful not to pierce the crust. Place the tomatoes, capsicum, olives and spring onions in a bowl. Season with salt and pepper and drizzle with vinaigrette. Layer the seasoned vegetables and the artichokes, egg and anchovy in the rolls, drizzling a little pistou between some of the layers. Press the lid back on the top of each roll and wrap firmly in cling wrap. The juice and dressing will be absorbed by the bread and the flavours will have merged by the time you arrive at your picnic spot.

Variation

The beauty of this picnic classic is that the ingredients can be varied to suit your own taste or the ingredients available and still taste great. Layer the ingredients into the rolls or a baguette and slice just before serving for a better presentation.

Tuna tartare

A tuna tartare with Japanese flavours. The wasabi tobiko which tops this dish is a beautiful crunchy texture that contrasts with the tuna and the soft avocado. The togarashi dressing increases the intensity of flavour. The natural flying fish roe is infused with wasabi which gives it the splendid green colour.

Ingredients

Togarashi dressing

2 teaspoons peeled and grated ginger

1 teaspoon minced garlic

2 red serrano or similar hot chillies, sliced, seeded and chopped

1½ tablespoons sesame oil

2 tablespoons peanut oil

2 tablespoons lime juice

1½ tablespoons soy sauce

1 teaspoon sugar

2 teaspoons togarashi (Japanese hot red chilli powder)

2 avocadoes, peeled, cut crosswise in 1 cm slices

650 g sashimi-quality tuna, trimmed, cut and diced carefully

1 Lebanese cucumber, peeled, seeded and diced

Pinch black sesame seeds

Pinch white sesame seeds

10 teaspoons wasabi tobiko (flying fish roe)

10 lime wedges

Serves 10

To make the togarashi dressing, place all the ingredients in a jar and shake well. Store in the refrigerator until needed. When using the dressing don't whisk or mix together because you want to serve the dressing unemulsified, but make sure you spoon through all the layers to get a balanced sauce.

To prepare the tuna, trim and cover in cling-wrap to keep it fresh. Chill the tuna well before dicing. With a very sharp knife, working quickly and cleanly, slice the tuna—do not chop it or the texture will be ruined.

To assemble the tuna tartare, use a cutter or pastry ring (60 mm round x 30 mm high). Line the base of the ring with the avocado slices. Top the avocado with diced raw tuna to fill the ring and level off the top. Place the ring of tartare in the centre of each serving plate and remove the metal ring.

Spoon a little togarashi dressing over the tartare. Add some of the cucumber dice on top of the tartare and sprinkle with the sesame seeds. Place a teaspoon of wasabi tobiko on top of the cucumber. Spoon some of the dressing onto the plate around the tuna tartare. Place a lime wedge at the back of the tartare and serve with thinly sliced toasted baguette and more dressing on the side.

SERVING TIP

Tuna tartare can be assembled in minutes with a little advance preparation. Dice the tuna and cucumber and keep them well chilled in separate airtight containers. Prepare the sauce. Just before your guests arrive, peel the avocadoes and line the moulds, cover with cling-wrap and keep well chilled. All the components are now ready. Allow your guests to add the salt and lime juice to their own tartare—adding these beforehand will leach out precious juices.

RIGHT: Tuna tartare

Dukkah

Dukkah is a spice mix which originated in Egypt—it is served throughout the day as a snack. It's perfect for a beach picnic.

Ingredients
Dukkah

1 ¾ cups sesame seeds

1 ½ cups coriander seeds

1 ½ cups white almond meal

½ cup ground cumin

1 teaspoon sea salt

½ teaspoon freshly ground black pepper

Crusty Italian-style bread or ciabatta

Extra-virgin olive oil

Serves 10

To make the dukkah, roast the sesame seeds on a small baking tray in a preheated oven at 175°C for 8 minutes, until aromatic. At the same time, roast the coriander seeds for 4 minutes on a separate tray and the almond meal for 5 minutes on a separate tray.

Remove from the oven and as they are ready place them in a large bowl. Add the cumin, salt and pepper and mix well. Blend the ingredients together in a food processor until they are finely crushed, but not as fine as a powder. The dukkah should be a crushed dry mixture, so don't overprocess or the oil from the sesame seeds and almond will turn it into a paste. Store in an airtight jar—it will keep for 3–4 weeks.

To serve the dukkah, place a small amount in a shallow bowl, place the olive oil in a small dish and slice the bread. Everyone dips the end of their bread into the oil and then into the dukkah and enjoys at their leisure.

Try sprinkling dukkah on grilled fish and serve with leeks, butter and lemon. It is also a good accompaniment for the Grilled asparagus with soft egg and croûtons (page 45).

Spicy green olives

A little blast at the beginning of the picnic to awaken the appetite. Serve with crusty bread and a small bowl of diced Preserved lemon peel (page 39) to balance the flavours.

Ingredients

1 ½ cups picholine or firm green olives

1 garlic clove, minced

1 red serrano or similar hot chilli, seeded and finely chopped

1 teaspoon coriander seeds, lightly crushed

¼ teaspoon ground cumin

3 tablespoons extra-virgin olive oil

To prepare the olives, drain them from their brine and rinse. Put them in a container, add the remaining ingredients, place the lid on and shake to mix well. Leave the olives to marinate for a few hours or refrigerate until needed. Return to room temperature before serving.

Buffalo milk mozzarella
with ox-heart tomatoes and olive salsa

A great name for a vegetarian entrée salad. Serve with lots of crusty bread to soak up the delicious juices.

Ingredients

Olive salsa

5 tablespoons stoned and coarsely chopped black olives

3 tablespoons stoned and coarsely chopped green olives

3 tablespoons finely chopped red onion

10 oven-dried cherry tomatoes, halved

1 red serrano or similar hot chilli, seeded, chopped

3 tablespoons tiny capers, rinsed

⅗ cup extra-virgin olive oil

4 tablespoons roughly chopped fresh flat-leaf parsley

6 ox-heart tomatoes, sliced

Sea salt and freshly ground black pepper

2 tablespoons red-wine vinegar

10 buffalo mozzarella, sliced

Serves 6

To prepare the salsa, mix all the ingredients and macerate for 30 minutes.

To serve, slice the ox-heart tomatoes and place around individual plates or a platter in an overlapping circle. Season the tomatoes with salt and pepper, drizzle with a little vinegar and spoon some salsa over the tomatoes. Form a circle in the centre of the tomatoes with the mozzarella slices and spoon more salsa over the cheese. Drizzle with extra olive oil if necessary.

VARIATIONS

The Olive salsa is very adaptable. Serve it with similar style dishes such as goat's cheese lightened with half its weight of ricotta and beaten together with a few fresh herbs. Either mould the cheese or just leave it to harden in the refrigerator before slicing it and serving with roasted tomatoes, artichokes and salsa. Grill rouget (red mullet) or swordfish and serve with Samfaina (page 25) and salsa. Fry or grill Polenta (page 133), top it with warmed Salt cod brandade (page 47) and serve it with the salsa.

Seared spice-crusted tuna
on soba and cucumber noodles

LEFT: Seared spice-crusted
tuna on soba and
cucumber noodles

A simple dish combining heat and cooling elements, all of which are balanced by interplaying flavours. The spice crust is very versatile and adds dimension to most tuna dishes. The dish requires good quality, very fresh tuna, which is available in Australia most of the time.

Ingredients

Spice mix

1 tablespoon black peppercorns

1 tablespoon white peppercorns

1½ tablespoons fennel seeds

2 tablespoons coriander seeds

1½ tablespoons sea salt

2 teaspoons cayenne pepper

1 tablespoon mustard seeds

Cucumber noodles

½ cup white-wine vinegar

3 tablespoons sugar

2 Lebanese cucumbers, seeded, shaved lengthwise

200 g soba noodles

Soy and ginger vinaigrette

½ cup extra-virgin olive oil

1½ tablespoons sesame oil

1½ tablespoons light soy sauce

2½ tablespoons lime juice, strained

2 teaspoons ginger, peeled, freshly grated

1–2 red serrano or similar hot chillies, seeded, chopped

Salt and freshly ground black pepper

1½ tablespoons boiling water

500 g sashimi-quality tuna loin, skin and dark roe removed

3 tablespoons fresh coriander leaves

Serves 4

To make the spice mix, blend all the ingredients together in a spice mill or blender until quite fine. You will have more than you need so keep some stored in an airtight jar in the refrigerator.

To make the cucumber noodles, combine the vinegar and sugar in a small stainless steel saucepan over a low heat, stirring occasionally, until the sugar has dissolved. Remove from the heat and cool to room temperature. Place the cucumbers in a bowl and marinate in the sauce for 30 minutes. Drain the cucumber.

Cook the soba noodles in plenty of boiling salted water for 3 minutes or until just tender to the tooth. Refresh in ice water and set aside.

To make the soy and ginger vinaigrette, combine all the ingredients in a bowl and whisk to blend. Place in an airtight jar and allow to settle.

To prepare the tuna loin, cut it in half lengthwise and then down the middle to make four equal sized pieces. Roll the tuna on all sides in the spice mixture.

Prepare a flat top grill to very hot and brush with a little oil. Sear the tuna quickly on each side just to colour and cook the outside, about 2 minutes. Remove from the grill and place on a cutting board in a warm place.

To serve, toss the soba noodles together in a bowl and add some vinaigrette to moisten. Place the mixture in the centre of serving bowls and spoon over more vinaigrette to moisten well. Top with most of the coriander leaves and the cucumber noodles. Slice each piece of tuna thinly into four or five pieces and overlap each portion on the cucumber noodles. Add more coriander leaves and serve with extra vinaigrette on the side.

Mussels and oysters

Two separate ideas for serving oysters and mussels—a mignonette sauce with the oysters and a simple grilling technique with lemon for the mussels—serve them on the same occasion! The only way to ensure you have the taste of the ocean with your oysters is to buy them either unopened or have them opened for you, just before you need them. It's best to avoid eating oysters in late summer—the oysters are spawning and milky tasting.

Ingredients

Mignonette sauce

¼ **cup red-wine vinegar**

1 tablespoon chopped green shallots

1 tablespoon chopped golden shallots

1 tablespoon black pepper, coarsely ground, sieved to remove dust

36 oysters, the best and freshest available

36 black mussels, tightly closed, cleaned and bearded (page 28)

1 lemon, cut into wedges

Serves 6

To make the mignonette sauce, mix the red-wine vinegar, green and golden shallots and black pepper together in a small bowl and either drizzle a little sauce over each oyster or serve the sauce separately to dip the oysters into.

To prepare the mussels, place them directly onto a very hot grill. They will open quickly and are ready as soon as they do. Remove from the grill plate with tongs onto a platter, squeeze with lemon juice and serve. Serve with all their juices and crusty wood-fired bread to mop them up.

Variation

Embellish the mussels with Pistou (page 29) or Lemon vinaigrette (page 129) mixed with chopped dill and finely diced fennel. Drizzle either dressing over the musssels as they come off the grill.

Samfaina

Samfaina is a Catalan variation of ratatouille. Here I have refined it further resulting in a completeness of flavour. It's one of my favourite accompaniments and has an infinite variety of uses. Serve with grilled sourdough as a spread, pita bread as a dip, or with grilled fish or lamb. Once you begin making it regularly you will find uses for it all the time. Serve at room temperature.

Ingredients

3 kg eggplants

3 tablespoons olive oil

1 kg onions, peeled, halved and very finely sliced

1.3 kg Roasted red capsicums (page 137), peeled, diced

5 teaspoons minced garlic cloves

16 anchovy fillets in oil, drained, minced

1 tablespoon ground cumin

1 tablespoon paprika

Sea salt and freshly ground black pepper

2 teaspoons ground coriander seed

3 tablespoons chopped fresh parsley

2 tablespoons chopped fresh basil

3 tablespoons good quality extra-virgin olive oil

Serves 10–15

To cook the eggplants, rub them with olive oil and cut off the tops. To help with even cooking, cut an incision-like cross at the top end of the eggplant, about 6 cm down, and wrap them securely in foil. Place on an oiled baking tray and bake in a preheated oven at 200°C for 20 minutes. Check that the eggplant are completely cooked and remove from the oven. Unwrap the eggplant, cut in half lengthwise and place vertically in a colander to drain while they cool.

Meanwhile, cover a heavy saucepan with a film of olive oil, add the onions, cover and sweat the onions over a very low heat and cook for about 10 minutes. Remove the lid to allow the onions to turn a little golden brown. Add the roasted capsicum dice, garlic, anchovies, cumin and paprika, and combine over a low heat for 5–6 minutes.

Scrape the eggplant flesh away from the skin with a spoon onto a chopping board. Chop the flesh up a little and add to the onion and capsicum mixture on the stove. Mix well and cook over a low heat for a few minutes to blend the flavours and cook down a little. Add a little olive oil if necessary, season with salt, pepper and coriander seed. Cool and refrigerate. Before using, return to room temperature and stir in the parsley and basil. Spoon into a bowl and drizzle with good extra-virgin olive oil. Samfaina will keep for 1 week, refrigerated.

COOKING EGGPLANTS
Eggplant should always be completely cooked. Undercooked eggplant attacks the palate with harsh bitter flavours which ruin the dish.

See photo page 134

On the verandah

Lunch and light meals

Fish and shellfish are perfect for light summer eating. They are my favourite food to cook because they offer great flexibility and their capacity to blend with exciting flavours seems endless.

Most seafood are a wild product so the quality of fish and shellfish are a constant variable. The finished dish will depend on the quality of your ingredients. Remember when selecting fish, fresh fish look and smell fresh—if you are in any doubt then it's not fresh. Fresh fish will have clear, bulging eyes, and the skin will have a bright natural sheen. The flesh should be firm and spring back when you press it. It should also smell of the sea and not fishy. As soon as you get it home, store it surrounded by, but not in, plenty of ice because fish is very delicate.

It is always best to buy whole fish but scaling, filleting and portioning fish at home can be a daunting task, so if you are not confident ask your fishmonger to do it for you. I like to trim fillets into neat similar-sized portions so the cooking times will be even. Some fish, such as Snapper and John Dory, benefit by a light scoring of the skin with the tip of a sharp knife. If fish is to be pan-seared, dry the skin well by dragging the back of a knife over the fish pressing down at the same time to release water from the skin. Wipe the fish with a dry tea towel and repeat a few more times and this will ensure the skin will be crisp before it is overcooked.

Knowing when fish is cooked takes some practice and experience. Look for a point on the side of the fish where you can see it turn from translucent to opaque. The flesh becomes firmer as it cooks but it should still 'give' a little when pressed, indicating it is not overcooked. Its own heat will complete the cooking when removed from the heat.

When you buy scallops on the half shell you will need to release the scallop from the shell. Working with a small knife, gently lift up and detach the muscle where it is attached to the shell. Keep the white muscle of the scallop and discard the rest. The scallop has a small attachment on the side— cut off and discard. Wipe the scallops gently with a tea towel and keep well chilled. Make sure they are very dry before cooking them.

RIGHT: Steamed mussels with saffron and dill (recipe overleaf)

Steamed mussels
with saffron and dill

Mussels are easy to prepare, they contain their own built-in stock and can be cooked in minutes. Don't reduce the sauce too much as you are aiming for a half soup, half sauce consistency. Always soak the saffron threads in a little warm water to infuse the colour before adding both saffron and water to your sauce, soup or stock. And remember, mussels love black pepper, but only add salt after you have determined how salty the mussel stock tastes.

Ingredients

2 kg black mussels

2 tablespoons unsalted butter

½ onion, finely sliced

2 teaspoons minced garlic

3 tablespoons white wine

½ cup cream

1 teaspoon saffron threads, diluted in 1½ tablespoons
warm water

1 carrot, peeled, julienned

1 leek, white part only, julienned

Sea salt and freshly ground black pepper

3 tablespoons fresh dill sprigs

2 teaspoons lemon juice

Serves 4

To prepare the mussels, first pull the beard threads off the mussels with your fingers. Give the shells a quick wash or scrub if they are dirty and discard any that are open. Melt the butter in a large, wide saucepan, add the onion and garlic and sweat for 2 minutes over a low heat to soften. Add the white wine and bring to a fast boil over a high heat. Tip in the mussels, cover with a tight-fitting lid and leave for about 2 minutes, shaking the pan vigorously from side to side occasionally. Remove the lid and take out any mussels that have just opened and leave to drain in a bowl. Replace the lid, give the pan a shake, open again and check the mussels—keep removing the mussels immediately after they open so they don't overcook but remain juicy and plump. Discard any mussels that remain closed.

To make the sauce, strain the juices released by the mussels through a very fine sieve, preferably lined with muslin cloth. Return the juice with an equal amount of water to the cleaned saucepan. Place over a high heat again, add the cream, saffron and saffron water, carrot, leek, salt and pepper and bring to a boil. Continue cooking for 2 minutes to reduce the sauce a little and allow the saffron to infuse its flavour. Add the dill and lemon juice to taste and adjust the seasoning (don't add too much salt as the mussel juice is already quite salty). Place the mussels back in the saucepan to give them a very quick reheat for half a minute.

To serve, divide the mussels among deep warm bowls with the sauce. Serve with light crusty bread to soak up the juices.

Salad of marron
with baby vegetables, herbs and pistou

A celebration of perfect ingredients—marron (freshwater crayfish) sits on a bed of steamed fresh vegetables topped with a light salad of herbs. Just right for a special lunch on the verandah. Steamed prawns also work well with this recipe. Pistou is a French version of pesto which comes from just over the border in Italy.

Ingredients

Pistou

½ **packed cup fresh green basil leaves**

½ **packed cup fresh flat-leaf parsley leaves**

½ **cup extra-virgin olive oil**

Sea salt and freshly ground black pepper

Court bouillon

1 onion, finely sliced

1 celery stalk, finely sliced

1 carrot, finely sliced

2 star anise

10 black peppercorns

6 fresh parsley stalks

3 fresh thyme sprigs

6 cups water

Peel of ½ lemon

½ **cup white wine**

6 250–g marrons, live

½ **bulb fennel, shaved lengthwise, blanched and refreshed**

½ **cup baby green beans, blanched and refreshed**

½ **cup green peas, blanched and refreshed**

¼ **cup snowpeas, julienned, blanched and refreshed**

3 tablespoons tomato, peeled, seeded and diced

Lemon vinaigrette (page 129)

Salad of herbs (page 139) or fresh chervil sprigs

Serves 6

See photo pages 2–3

To make the pistou, blanch the parsley and basil for 15 seconds in boiling water. Remove from the water and plunge into iced water to refresh quickly. As soon as the leaves are cool, drain them well. Place the drained leaves in a dry towel and squeeze well to remove all the moisture. The leaves must be very dry.

Place the leaves in a blender or food processor with half of the oil and purée well while adding the remaining oil in a steady stream. Season lightly with salt and pepper and reserve in an airtight container.

To make the court bouillon, place all the ingredients except the wine in a stainless steel saucepan and cover with the water. Bring to the boil and simmer for 15 minutes. Add the wine, bring back to the boil and simmer for 1 minute.

Before cooking the marrons, put them in the freezer to stun them. Then put the marrons into the simmering court bouillon and cook for 8 minutes. Remove and leave to cool. Before serving, carefully remove the meat from their tail shells, and slice lengthwise.

Mix the shaved fennel, beans, peas, snowpeas and tomato dice together in a bowl and toss with some of the lemon vinaigrette. Toss the marrons with the lemon vinaigrette in a bowl and season with salt and pepper.

To serve, drain the vegetables of excess dressing and divide among 6 plates. Arrange the marrons on the vegetables and add a little more dressing as needed. Spoon some of the pistou on the plates around the salads and toss the herb salad with a little lemon vinaigrette. Place a decorative pile of herb salad on top of the marrons and serve.

Linguine with prawns,

snowpeas, peas and lemon

Pasta for a light summer lunch.

Ingredients

400 g dried linguine

3 tablespoons extra-virgin olive oil

24 prawns, shelled, de-veined (page 141)

1⅕ cups Lemon vinaigrette (page 129)

½ cup fresh peas

30 snowpeas, julienned, blanched, refreshed

**1½ teaspoons red serrano or similar hot chillies, seeded,
finely chopped**

2 teaspoons minced garlic

3 tablespoons coarsely chopped fresh flat-leaf parsley

1 tablespoon fresh basil leaves, coarsely torn

Sea salt and freshly ground black pepper

Serves 6

To cook the linguine, place it in a saucepan with at least 5 litres of boiling salted water. Cook at a rapid boil until al dente, about 7–8 minutes, or according to the packet instructions. Drain, but always leave a little of the cooking water with the pasta to help it integrate with the sauce and garnish.

Meanwhile, heat the extra-virgin olive oil in a large frying pan over a high heat. Add the prawns and cook quickly on each side, keeping them translucent in the centre. Lower the heat and add the lemon vinaigrette, peas, snowpeas, chilli, garlic and herbs and cook together for about 1 minute to heat through. Add the cooked linguine, toss and mix through the prawns and vegetables. Season with salt and pepper.

To serve, divide the pasta between warm bowls, placing the prawns near the top of each serving.

LEFT: Linguine with prawns, snowpeas, peas and lemon

RIGHT: Panfried reef snapper with tapenade, leeks and tomato (recipe overleaf)

Panfried reef snapper
with tapenade, leeks and tomato

Reef snapper, goldband snapper or rosy jobfish as it should be called, is a great fish for pan frying. Partnered here with tapenade, young leeks, tomato and herbs it's a quick dish to put together and reflects the lightness of summer.

Ingredients

Tapenade

500 g kalamata olives

100 g anchovy fillets, rinsed

2 tablespoons small salted capers, rinsed

1 garlic clove

4 tablespoons extra-virgin olive oil

Freshly ground black pepper

Tomato dressing

4 egg-shaped (roma) tomatoes, peeled, seeded, diced, and well drained

1 golden shallot, peeled, finely chopped

2 tablespoons chopped fresh flat-leaf parsley

2 tablespoons chopped fresh chervil

2 tablespoons chopped fresh tarragon

6 fennel seeds

12 coriander seeds, crushed

Sea salt and freshly ground black pepper

1¾ cups extra-virgin olive oil

1½ tablespoons lemon juice, strained

3 tablespoons olive oil

6 150–g rosy jobfish or snapper, skin on, cleaned, well dried

12 baby leeks, blanched, refreshed

1 lemon, cut into wedges

Serves 6

To make the tapenade, stone the olives, rinse, drain and place in a food processor with the anchovies, capers and garlic. Blend while adding the olive oil in a stream with pepper. Tapenade will keep for weeks if stored in an airtight container and refrigerated, and is a great condiment to have on hand.

To make the tomato dressing, place the tomatoes, shallots, herbs and spices in a bowl. Season with salt and pepper and stir in the olive oil and lemon juice. Leave to marinate for 10 minutes.

To cook the fish, make sure the fish is well dried on the skin side, and season lightly. Heat the olive oil in a teflon-coated pan and place the fillet skin side down into the hot frying pan and press down on the fish with a metal spatula to keep the fish flat. Cook until the skin and flesh is a nice golden colour on this first side, about 3 minutes, then turn the heat to low and turn the fish over. Complete the cooking over a low heat for a minute or two, remove from the pan and keep warm. Repeat this process with the remaining fish. Meanwhile reheat the leeks, by steaming them for 1 minute.

To serve, place the the leeks in the centre of warm serving plates. Spoon the tomato dressing over the leeks and top with the fish, skin side up. Spread an even layer of tapenade over the fish and serve with lemon wedges.

Grilled white scallops,
asparagus, fennel and orange

A perfect blend of flavours for early summer—the orange acts as a balance to the scallops and both harmonise with the asparagus and fennel. The secret to grilling the scallops is to have the grill or pan very hot, and not to turn the scallops until they have formed a golden colour on the first side and are nearly cooked through.

Ingredients

Sauce

3 fresh oranges, juiced, strained

1 tablespoon lemon juice, strained

1 teaspoon dried chilli, flaked

50 g unsalted butter

Sea salt and freshly ground black pepper

1 fennel bulb

½ cup Lemon vinaigrette (page 129)

12 asparagus, peeled, blanched for 3 minutes, refreshed, halved

⅓ cup landcress or curly endive, optional

24 white scallops, trimmed

2 tablespoons olive oil

1 tablespoon fresh dill fronds

Serves 6

To prepare the sauce, place the orange juice, lemon juice and chilli in a stainless steel saucepan over a medium heat. Reduce to ⅓ cup, about 15 minutes. Remove from the heat and whisk in the butter and season with salt and pepper. Strain the sauce into a small saucepan. Reserve in a warm place.

To prepare the salad, trim any damaged outside ribs off the fennel. Cut it in half lengthwise and shave very finely on a sharp mandoline. Toss the fennel in some lemon vinaigrette and season with salt and pepper. Place a small pile of fennel in the centre of each plate and top with the asparagus. Drizzle a little more vinaigrette over the asparagus and top with a little landcress, if liked.

To cook the scallops, heat a flat-top grill or a teflon frying pan over a high heat to very hot. Brush with the olive oil. Add the scallops and cook on the first side until lightly caramelised to a nice golden colour, about 2 minutes. Turn the scallops over and cook for another 30 seconds. They will not take long and should remain moist in the middle. Remove the scallops to a warm plate and season with salt and pepper.

To serve, reheat the sauce very gently if needed, and spoon it around the fennel salad on each plate. Place the scallops on the sauce around the salad and sprinkle with dill fronds. Drizzle any remaining scallop juices over and serve.

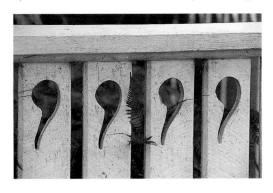

Seared tuna minute

with roasted tomato, caper and olive salsa

A great idea, achieved in minutes—searing the tuna on one side only ensures it is presented as it should be—moist and pink.

Ingredients

Tomato, caper and olive salsa

24 cherry tomatoes, halved, oven-dried (page 136)

6 teaspoons tiny salted capers, rinsed

6 teaspoons stoned and sliced black olives

3 tablespoons chopped fresh flat-leaf parsley

3/5 cup Lemon vinaigrette (page 129)

1 tablespoon sea salt

Freshly ground black pepper

1 red serrano or similar hot chilli, seeded, finely chopped

3 tablespoons Tapenade (page 32)

6 100–g sashimi-quality tuna slices, cut thinly (1 cm deep) and evenly across the fillet

1 cup landcress, watercress or lamb's lettuce (mâche)

1/2 cup curly endive, white part only

2 tablespoons Lemon vinaigrette

1 lemon, cut in wedges

Serves 6

To make the salsa, mix the roasted tomatoes, capers, olives and chopped parsley together in a bowl with enough lemon vinaigrette to moisten well. Season and add chilli to taste. Leave aside for 15 minutes.

Spoon a little tapenade onto each plate. Season the tuna on one side only with black pepper and sear quickly on a very hot flat grill plate. The tuna is only cooked on this one side so sear it well until the side begins to colour a little. Remove the tuna from the grill and place on the tapenade and spoon some roasted tomato salsa on top of each portion of the tuna. Toss the salads with a little vinaigrette and place a small mound on top of the salsa and tuna. Drizzle with a little more vinaigrette and serve with lemon wedges.

VARIATIONS

Search for the freshest, highest quality tuna when serving it raw or lightly cooked. Vary the flavouring ingredients of the recipe above by adding capsicums, beans, fennel and so on. For added zest try sprinkling one side of the tuna with Tuna spice mix (page 23) before sealing it.

RIGHT: Seared tuna minute with roasted tomato, caper and olive salsa

Polenta with grilled tomatoes,
prosciutto and buffalo milk mozzarella

A light delicious lunch. Polenta is a wonderful vehicle for highly flavoured foods. Here the warmth of the polenta helps to soften the mozzarella and the tomato, prosciutto and basil integrate all their flavours.

Ingredients

Set polenta (page 133)

8 ripe egg-shaped (roma) tomatoes

Sea salt and freshly ground black pepper

½ cup extra-virgin olive oil

2 garlic cloves, finely sliced

3 tablespoons flour

4 buffalo milk mozzarella, sliced

8 slices prosciutto

16 fresh basil leaves

Serves 4

To prepare the polenta, follow the instructions on page 133 for set polenta. When firm, cut the polenta into 4 large or 8 small rectangular or triangular pieces. Preheat the flat grill top to hot.

To prepare the tomatoes, core them, cut them in half and scoop out the seeds. Season the tomatoes with salt and pepper, drizzle with a little olive oil and sprinkle the garlic slices over them.

To cook the polenta and tomatoes, paint the hot grill with olive oil and put the seasoned tomatoes on top. Toss the polenta with flour, shake off any excess and place on the hot grill. Turn the polenta once it has started to take on a golden colour and become crusted, and repeat on the second side. Cook the tomatoes until they begin to collapse and turn them over to finish cooking.

To serve the polenta and tomatoes, remove the polenta from the grill and place on warm plates. Top with the slices of mozzarella and place the tomatoes on the mozzarella. Drape the prosciutto over the tomatoes and sprinkle over the basil leaves. Drizzle with more olive oil and grind with pepper.

MOZZARELLA

Mozzarella was originally made from buffalo not cow's milk in Italy. It has a more refined flavour and an intense aroma which make it well worth the extra expense.

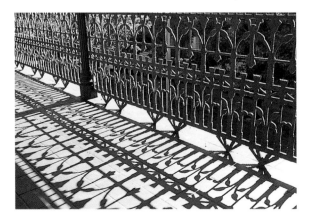

Oven-steamed salmon
on almond tarator with caper and vegetable salsa

Tarator is a heady Turkish sauce usually based on walnuts. I've used almond instead for a more subtle combination with the moist salmon. The caper and vegetable salsa lifts and brings the dish together—a great interplay of flavours and cultures.

Ingredients

5 200–g salmon fillets, skin on, and pin bones removed

¾ **cup Lebanese cucumber, peeled, julienned or finely shaved on a mandoline slicer**

5 tablespoons Lemon vinaigrette (page 129)

Almond tarator sauce (page 128)

½ **cup endive salad, white inner leaves only**

½ **cup fresh chervil sprigs, picked and washed**

¼ **cup snipped fresh dill**

½ **cup Caper and vegetable salsa (page 137)**

Serves 10

To oven-steam the salmon, preheat the oven to 90°C. Place a baking tray of boiling water on the bottom of the oven and arrange an oven rack on the top half of the oven. Butter a flat metal baking sheet, put the salmon on top and place the sheet on the upper rack in the oven. Oven-steam for about 15–20 minutes. The low temperature will ensure the fat content of the salmon just sets—it should remain very moist and juicy and not lose much of its original colour.

Meanwhile, mix the julienned or shaved cucumber with a little of the lemon vinaigrette and season with black pepper—don't use any salt.

Check the tarator sauce—if it is too thick, whisk in a little water to lighten. Place a small portion of the cucumber on the plate and spoon over a tablespoon of almond tarator.

To make a herb salad, toss the curly endive, chervil and dill in a bowl with a little lemon vinaigrette and divide into ten small piles. When the salmon is ready, remove from the oven and carefully transfer each piece to a chopping board. Prepare quickly while the salmon is still warm. Turn the salmon over in your hand and remove the skin—it should peel away easily. Place back on the board and cut each piece horizontally into two. Repeat with the remaining fillets.

To serve, place a piece of salmon on top of the cucumber and tarator sauce on each plate. Spoon over the caper and vegetable salsa and top each salmon with a pile of prepared herb salad.

The salmon can be cooked earlier and either served at room temperature or quickly reheated to only just warm, for a few minutes in a preheated oven at 100°C.

OVEN STEAMING

Oven steaming (and confit where the salmon is submerged in olive oil and cooked at a very low temperature) has become very popular over the past 10 years. It is perfect for cooking salmon as it produces a very moist, tender flesh full of natural flavour. It conserves all the natural oils inside the fish which tend to leach out when the fish is cooked with fierce heat.

See photo page 127

Blue-eye cod fillet
on white beans, roast tomatoes
and preserved lemons

A combination of Mediterranean flavours which suit the moist flesh of blue-eye cod. Italians love the combination of white beans with seafood. Swordfish or mahi mahi would be just as delicious.

Ingredients
Preserved lemons
10 lemons
1²⁄₃ cups sea salt
1½ cups lemon juice
Olive oil

Anchovy vinaigrette
12 anchovy fillets
1½ tablespoons sherry vinaigrette (page 129)
1 tablespoon fresh rosemary leaves
³⁄₅ cup extra-virgin olive oil
Freshly ground black pepper

3 tablespoons olive oil
Sea salt and freshly ground black pepper
6 180–g blue-eye cod fillets
1 cup cannellini beans, cooked (see chickpeas page 63)
6 oven-dried tomatoes, halved, sliced lengthwise
1 Roasted red capsicum (page 137), julienned
4 tablespoons small black olives
2 tablespoons fresh flat-leaf parsley, coarsely chopped
1 tablespoon Preserved lemon (above), diced

Serves 6

LEFT: Blue-eye cod fillet on white beans, roast tomatoes and preserved lemons

To prepare the preserved lemons, wash and dry the lemons. Cut them into 8 wedges and squeeze the wedges to obtain the juice. Toss the lemons with salt and place in a glass jar. Pour in the lemon juice. Make extra if the juice of 10 lemons isn't enough. Close the jar tightly, and let the lemons ripen at room temperature for 7 days, shaking the jar each day to distribute the salt and juice. To store, float the olive oil on top of the lemon juices, and refrigerate for up to 6 months.

To use, remove the lemons as needed from the jar. Remove the flesh and most of the pith and cut the lemon rind into dice. Use as directed by the recipe or place in a bowl in the centre of the table for people to nibble on throughout the meal.

To make the anchovy vinaigrette, place all the ingredients in a blender and purée well. Remove and set aside.

To cook the blue-eye cod, heat the olive oil in a frying pan over a high heat. Season the fish and cook the blue-eye cod until it begins to look a golden colour, about 4 minutes, before turning. Lower the heat, turn the fish over and cook a little longer. Tip the oil from the pan and place the pan and fish in a preheated oven at 200°C to finish cooking for a few minutes.

Meanwhile, mix the cannellini beans, tomato, roasted capsicum, olives and parsley in a bowl and toss with a little anchovy vinaigrette to moisten.

To serve, spoon 3 tablespoons of this mixture onto the centre of the plates. Remove the fish from the oven and place on top of the salad. Season with more anchovy vinaigrette, the diced preserved lemon and season with pepper.

Eggplant and chicken curry
with grilled chicken

Don't be put off by the long list of ingredients you find for most curries. You'll be surprised—it actually only takes minutes to assemble the ingredients.

Ingredients

700 g eggplant, cut into 2 cm dice

1 tablespoon sea salt

2 tablespoons brown mustard seeds

½ cup olive oil

Curry base

2 onions, finely sliced

3 tablespoons olive oil

2 tablespoons minced garlic

1½ tablespoons peeled and grated ginger

1 tablespoon ground cumin

½ teaspoon ground cardamom

½ teaspoon ground coriander

½ teaspoon cayenne pepper

½ teaspoon tumeric

½ teaspoon fenugreek seeds

3 cloves

3 egg-shaped (roma) tomatoes, peeled, seeded, diced

1 tablespoon sugar

1½ cups water

8 150–g chicken breasts, wings trimmed, skin on

Sea salt and freshly ground black pepper

500 g spinach, washed

Serves 8

To cook the eggplant, toss it in the salt, place in a colander and leave to drain for 30 minutes. Give the eggplant a quick rinse and dry well in a tea towel. Meanwhile, place the mustard seeds in a frying pan over a moderate heat and roast until they begin popping. Remove the pan and reserve. Heat the olive oil in a large frying pan over a high heat and add the dried eggplant. Sauté, stirring frequently, until the eggplant are lightly browned on all sides and well cooked. Add the mustard seeds to the eggplant, give it a good stir and turn it out into a bowl and reserve.

To prepare the curry base, sweat the onions in the olive oil in a saucepan over a low heat until they soften a little, about 3 minutes. Raise the heat to medium and sauté the onions, stirring frequently until they are golden brown, about 5 minutes. Add the garlic and ginger and cook for 1 minute to release their flavours, then add all the spices and cook for another minute, stirring constantly. Add the tomatoes, sugar and water, raise the heat to high and bring to the boil. Lower the heat and simmer for 3 minutes. Remove and reserve.

To cook the chicken, preheat a flat grill or barbecue plate. Sprinkle the chicken breasts with salt and grill, skin side down for 3–4 minutes. Check the chicken and continue cooking for 2–3 minutes. Turn the chicken over and cook until it begins to feel firm, about 3 minutes. Remove the chicken to a flat tray and cover well to rest and finish cooking.

Meanwhile, to finish the spinach and eggplant curry, add the eggplant and mustard seeds to the curry base. Heat a large Teflon frying pan over a high heat and add the spinach and cook down, stirring frequently. Continue cooking until all the spinach water has evaporated and add to the eggplant and curry mixture. Stir to mix all the ingredients together and heat through over a medium heat.

To serve the curry, divide it between warm plates. Cut the chicken breasts into 3 pieces and place a breast on each curry. Sprinkle with sea salt.

Lemon ricotta and rocket tortellini
with asparagus and parmesan

A classic tortellini. Mixing the truffle oil into the lemon vinaigrette, allows its sometimes overpowering flavour to blend with the dish evenly.

Ingredients

Tortellini filling

500 g spinach leaves, washed

200 g rocket leaves, washed

900 g fresh ricotta

2 60–g eggs

Grated zest of ½ lemon

Sea salt and freshly ground black pepper

Pinch of grated nutmeg

2 quantities Ravioli pasta sheets (page 134)

30 asparagus spears, peeled

1 tablespoon white truffle oil

1 cup Lemon vinaigrette (page 129)

½ cup Clarified butter (page 128), warm

3 tablespoons finely grated parmesan cheese

Serves 10

To make the tortellini filling, cook the spinach and rocket in a large saucepan of boiling water, over a high heat for about 2 minutes. Remove the greens immediately with a large strainer and refresh them in iced water. Move the spinach around in the iced water to chill it quickly. Remove the spinach from the water and squeeze dry by hand. When most of the water has been removed, place the greens on a clean dry tea towel and squeeze all the remaining water from the greens. The secret to the filling is having the greens completely dry. Place the greens in the food processor or blender and chop well. Add a little ricotta and blend well. Add the remaining ricotta and blend again. Lastly put the eggs, zest, salt, pepper and nutmeg in the mixture and complete the blending. Place the tortellini filling in a bowl in the refrigerater, covered, for 1 hour to chill and firm up.

To form the tortellini, lay a prepared pasta sheet out flat along the bench. Place a half tablespoon of prepared filling evenly spaced for each tortellini down the upper side of each pasta sheet. Brush around each filling lightly with a little water to help it seal properly. Pick the lower edge of the pasta up between your fingers and fold it over the filling to make a package. Use the sides of your cupped hands to press down and seal the pasta. Using a 6 cm round cutter, stamp, seal and remove any air pockets. Take each semi-circle of pasta in your hand and curl the two ends of the straight edge around your finger pressing well to seal together. Repeat, and store in the refrigerator between dry tea towels.

To assemble, cook the asparagus in boiling salted water over a high heat, for about 3 minutes. Mix the truffle oil with the lemon vinaigrette, meanwhile cook the tortellini in boiling salted water for 2 minutes. Remove the asparagus, drain well and place on a chopping board. Remove the tips of each spear and dice the remainder of the stalk. Place the tips and spears on a hot plate or tray, season and brush with plenty of clarified butter. Keep warm. Remove the tortellini and drain.

To serve, divide the diced asparagus stalks between the bowls and top with the tortellini. Sprinkle on the asparagus spears, moisten with lemon vinaigrette and season with black pepper. Sprinkle with grated parmesan and serve.

From the garden

Salads and vegetables

Good food depends almost entirely on good produce. Australia is blessed with a vast range of the finest food ingredients. Developing a good relationship with your fruit and vegetable providore will repay that interest many times over. Demand the best and you will get to know a lot about fine flavour. Always choose beautiful, fresh produce that excites you—freshly picked and just opened zucchini flowers, smooth shiny capsicums or plump, fresh borlotti beans are always inspiring and make you feel like cooking.

A bowl of young, colourful salad leaves, lightly dressed with a balanced vinaigrette just before serving will delight and revive the most jaded palate. When buying your salads aim for a mixture such as curly endive, watercress, rocket, red and green oakleaf, mâche, radicchio and cos lettuce as well as a few herbs such as parsley, dill and chervil. The secret to a great salad is taking the care to use only the freshest, most tender leaves and herbs. Pick over your salads and discard any tough, bruised and wilted outside leaves. Break the inside leaves into small pieces as this will give you a taste of many flavours. Salad leaves are delicate and require gentle handling. Wash carefully in a large bowl of water and dry them well, preferably with a gentle motion in a salad spinner. Keep the salads refrigerated in a crisper container lined with a tea towel.

Throughout this book the terms, 'blanched, refreshed and drained' appear after many of the vegetables listed in the ingredients. Green beans and asparagus spears need to be quickly cooked in *plenty* of *salty* water in a *large* saucepan then refreshed so they remain green once they have cooked. Refresh them in *lots* of *iced* water until *well* chilled and then drain. A simple technique, especially useful when preparing a dish ahead of time. It's these details that are reflected in the flavour.

Many of the recipes in this chapter are full of helpful techniques, such as the Potato salad, Gazpacho, Brandade, Potato galette, Polenta, Poached eggs and Oven-dried tomatoes. Mastering a few basics allows your imagination greater freedom and gives you the confidence to experiment with cooking.

RIGHT: Salad of endives, Williams pear, gorgonzola and pecans (recipe overleaf)

Salad of endives, Williams pear,
gorgonzola and pecans

I love the contrasting flavours, textures and colours of this salad. There are rich, bitter, salty, cool and hot flavours—all combining to produce a classic mixture of tastes. Williams pears remind us that autumn is just around the corner.

Ingredients

Blue cheese vinaigrette

2 tablespoons gorgonzola cheese

½ cup Red-wine vinaigrette (page 129)

2 red witlof, leaves separated

2 white witlof, leaves separated

1 cup curly endive, white part only

1 cup watercress, picked and washed

½ cup gorgonzola cheese, broken into small pieces

3 Williams pears, peeled, and seeded, cut into quarters and sliced across

24 pecan nuts, toasted lightly, broken into halves

½ cup Red-wine vinaigrette

Serves 6

To make the blue cheese vinaigrette, place the gorgonzola and vinaigrette in a blender and purée until smooth. It will be quite thick. Set aside.

To make the endive salad, it's better to divide the ingredients between 2 or 3 large bowls for tossing together so you don't bruise the ingredients. Place the witlof leaves, endive, watercress, gorgonzola, Williams pears and pecan nuts in the large bowls. Add the blue cheese vinaigrette over the ingredients with a little red-wine vinaigrette as well. Toss together to lightly coat the ingredients and divide among the six bowls. Serve immediately.

Grilled asparagus
with soft egg and croûtons

Grilling or roasting asparagus after blanching them first, adds an extra flavour dimension. The soft poached egg doubles as a sauce and the croûtons add texture and balance. A great combination.

Ingredients

6 eggs, very fresh

½ teaspoon white-wine vinegar

½ cup olive oil

1 garlic clove, sliced

⅓ loaf sourdough or crusty Italian-style bread, crusts removed, cut into small cubes

30 green asparagus spears, ends cut off and peeled to 5 cm from the tip

Sea salt and freshly ground black pepper

2 tablespoons Clarified butter (page 128)

3 tablespoons Lemon vinaigrette (page 129)

1½ tablespoons parmesan cheese, finely sliced or grated

1 tablespoon snipped fresh chives

Serves 6

To poach the eggs you must first obtain very fresh eggs. Poaching anything that is not very fresh will not work as well. The whites should be firm near the yolks and form two distinct sections. Bring a deep saucepan of water to the boil and add the vinegar. Crack the eggs open and place on a small side plate or saucer. Once the water is simmering, stir the water to create a whirlpool effect and add the eggs two at a time. The swirling and depth of the water combine to help the white encircle the yolk and form its 'comet' shape. Poach for 2 minutes so the yolk will remain runny, and remove with a slotted spoon to a bowl of ice water to refresh. Once cool, remove, drain and cut off their flowing ponytails with scissors. The eggs will keep refrigerated in fresh water for a few days.

To make the croûtons, heat ½ cup of olive oil in a frying pan, add the garlic, then fry the croûtons until they are golden brown. Remove and drain on absorbent paper. Keep aside.

To cook the asparagus, blanch it in a large pot of boiling salted water for 2 minutes, remove, refresh in a bowl of iced water, and drain well to dry. Preheat the grill plate and paint with a little oil. Place the asparagus on the grill and allow to colour a little before turning. Continue cooking and turning until the asparagus are ready, about 2 minutes. Remove them to a tray with tongs, season well and brush liberally with clarified butter and lemon vinaigrette, sprinkle with grated parmesan and reserve in a warm place. Meanwhile, reheat the eggs for 1 minute in a saucepan of boiling water.

To serve, place 5 asparagus spears on each plate, sprinkle over the croûtons and spoon on some of the dressings from the asparagus. Place a warmed egg on each asparagus pile, season with salt and pepper and sprinkle the egg with the chives.

Zucchini flowers stuffed with brandade,
cherry tomato coulis

LEFT: Zucchini flowers stuffed with brandade, cherry tomato coulis

Zucchini flowers are a wonderful vehicle for many kinds of delicious stuffings. You will need to think ahead when using brandade as the salt cod needs to soak in water for at least one day. Check the balance of seasonings and flavorings before serving—it's important to bring the full depth of flavours out.

Ingredients

Salt cod brandade

250 g salt cod, soaked overnight or up to 2 days in water, trimmed

2 bay leaves

⅓ cup extra-virgin oil

100 g bintje potatoes (or any waxy variety), peeled, boiled, sieved to purée

1½ teaspoons minced garlic

½ cup double cream

Freshly ground black pepper

1 tablespoon lemon juice

Cherry tomato coulis

1 punnet cherry tomatoes

1 teaspoon sugar

Sea salt and freshly ground black pepper

24 zucchini flowers with zucchini attached

2 tablespoons Pistou (page 29)

Olive oil

Fresh chervil sprigs

Serves 6

TIP
Brandade and this cherry tomato coulis taste great served with grilled or fried polenta—good for a starter or light meal and another way to use these wonderful flavours.

To make the brandade, rinse the salt cod. In a heavy-bottomed saucepan over a high heat boil 4 cups of water with the bay leaves. Turn down the heat to very low or about 90°C. Add the cod and poach for 10 minutes making sure the water never boils, or the cod will be tough and stringy. Remove the cod once it is cooked and drain. Remove the skin and any bones and place the cod in a saucepan with the olive oil. Place over a low heat and beat the cod and oil together to break up the cod. Add the puréed potatoes and beat again. Remove this mixture to a food processor and add the garlic, cream and black pepper. Using the pulse button, blend together while adding the lemon juice. Season to taste with pepper—it may not need salt, and adjust the lemon juice if needed. Remove and cool.

To make the cherry tomato coulis, place the cherry tomatoes in a blender and purée until completely collapsed and puréed. Place a strainer over a stainless steel saucepan and pour the puréed tomatoes into the strainer. Push the tomatoes through the sieve to extract all the juice, and discard any pulp and seed. Add the sugar and a little salt and pepper to the tomato juices and bring to the boil over a medium heat. Scrape down the sides, lower the heat and simmer, reducing the purée to a sauce consistency. Remove from the heat, taste for seasoning and keep warm or reheat later when needed.

To prepare the zucchini flowers, open the flower and remove the stigmas. Spoon the brandade into the zucchini flowers until half full. Fold over the ends and tuck them under. Place the flowers end on end in the top of a steamer basket.

To serve, steam the zucchini flowers for 2–3 minutes to heat through. Meanwhile reheat the tomato sauce and place some in the centre of each plate. Spoon in a little pistou through the tomato sauce and top with four zucchini flowers per plate. Drizzle over a little olive oil and season with black pepper and chervil.

Linguine with summer vegetables,
pine nuts and herbs

In this light-but-tasty pasta dish I have cut the vegetables to resemble the linguine—it gives a harmonious visual effect.

Ingredients

250 g zucchini

1 white radish

2 tablespoons extra-virgin olive oil

5 tablespoons pine nuts

350 g dried linguine

3 tablespoons unsalted butter

6 oven-dried tomatoes, thinly sliced lengthwise

2 tablespoons thinly sliced green shallots

2 tablespoons chopped fresh flat-leaf parsley

2 tablespoons chopped fresh chervil

1 tablespoon fresh chives, cut in 5 cm lengths

2 tablespoons Lemon vinaigrette (page 129)

Sea salt and freshly ground black pepper

4 tablespoons parmesan cheese, finely grated

Serves 4

To prepare the vegetables, slice the zucchini lengthwise on a mandoline slicer which is set with the julienne blade. Discard the seedy middle of the zucchini. Peel the white radish and slice lengthwise into julienne on the same blade of the mandoline. Blanch the vegetables, one at a time in boiling salted water, cooking each vegetable for 1 minute. Drain, refresh in iced water and dry well. Place both vegetables in a bowl and set aside.

Heat 2 tablespoons of olive oil in a frying pan over a medium heat and cook the pine nuts until they begin to colour. Remove, drain and reserve.

Cook the linguine in plenty of boiling salted water in a large saucepan over a high heat until al dente, about 5–7 minutes or according to the packet instructions. Drain.

To serve, heat 3 tablespoons of butter in a large frying pan over a low heat and add the zucchini, radish, tomatoes, pine nuts and green shallots and heat gently for 1 minute. Add the drained linguine, the herbs, lemon vinaigrette and taste for salt and pepper. Mix the ingredients by tossing them together for 30 seconds and when the linguine has heated through divide among warm serving bowls. Serve with parmesan on the side.

Fresh vegetable soup
with summer herbs

A simple soup full of subtle and satisfying fresh flavours—essentially a way of using whatever vegetables are the best and freshest. The short cooking time ensures the fresh flavour of the individual vegetables is maintained. Cut the vegetables quite small so all their sweetness is extracted while sweating them. Add the herbs at the last minute to retain their fresh flavour.

Ingredients

50 g unsalted butter

2 carrots, peeled, cut into 5 mm dice

2 stalks celery, cut into 5 mm dice

1 leek, cut into 5 mm dice

4 golden shallots or 1 onion, finely chopped

2½ litres (10 cups) chicken stock (page 131)

Sea salt and freshly ground black pepper

1 cup green peas

1 cup green beans, 5 mm dice

1 cup broccoli, cut into very small florets

3 zucchini, cut into 5 mm dice

3 tablespoons chopped fresh chervil leaves

2 tablespoons chopped fresh flat-leaf parsley

Serves 8

To prepare the soup, place the butter in a large stainless steel saucepan over a low heat. Add the carrots, celery, leeks and shallots, cover, and sweat the vegetables for 3 minutes until they soften. Add the stock, salt and pepper and bring to the boil over a medium low heat so the vegetables will maintain their shape. Lower the heat and simmer the vegetables for 10 minutes to infuse their flavour. Increase the heat to medium high and add the peas, beans, broccoli and cook for another 2 minutes. Add the zucchini and cook for 1 minute. Taste the soup for seasoning, add the fresh herbs, give a final boil and remove from the heat.

To serve the soup, ladle into individual soup bowls dividing the vegetables, stock and herbs equally between the bowls.

Sweating the Vegetables

The technique of sweating the vegetables at the beginnng of this soup transforms their raw, harsher flavours. The vegetables' sweet flavours emerge as they soften in a small amount of butter over a very low heat. Cover the vegetables with a lid as they cook to promote the sweating and control their even cooking. The vegetables should not take on any colour. The butter will absorb all the vegetable flavours which in turn will be infused into the soup, sauce or stew.

Dicing Leeks

To dice a leek finely, cut a trimmed leek into 6 mm lengths with a sharp chef's knife. Cut a length vertically half through. Open it out flat on the board and dice.

Jalapeno-infused gazpacho

with avocado, blue swimmer crab and coriander

All the flavours of summer in one bowl. A refreshing starter or light lunch combining the best summer produce prepared with a little zing.

Ingredients

Gazpacho

1 teaspoon chopped garlic

1 red jalapeno or similar medium hot chilli, seeded and diced

2 Lebanese cucumbers, peeled, seeded, diced

1 red capsicum, diced

1½ kg ripe egg-shaped (roma) tomatoes, cored and diced

1 tablespoon sea salt or to taste

½ teaspoon white pepper, milled

4½ tablespoons sherry vinegar

½ cup extra-virgin olive oil

1 avocado, peeled

3 drops Tabasco sauce

Sea salt and freshly ground black pepper

150 g blue swimmer crab meat, shelled

2 tablespoons fresh coriander leaves, chopped

1 tablespoon Lemon vinaigrette (page 129)

½ red capsicum, fine short julienne

½ yellow capsicum, fine short julienne

1 Lebanese cucumber, fine short julienne

2 tablespoons fresh coriander leaves or sprigs

Extra-virgin olive oil

Serves 6

To prepare the gazpacho, place all the soup ingredients in a blender and purée well until finely blended. Remove and pass through a strainer, then pass the soup again through a very fine-meshed strainer. Correct the seasoning and refrigerate the soup for several hours until it is well chilled.

Mash the avocado in a bowl and season it with the Tabasco, salt and pepper. Place a small 3–4 cm pastry ring or cutter in the centre of a soup bowl and fill two-thirds with the avocado purée. Toss the blue swimmer crab meat with a little chopped coriander and the lemon vinaigrette in a bowl and place on top of the avocado. Decorate the crab with a little mixture of the capsicum and cucumber julienne and top with coriander leaves or sprigs. Repeat with the other five bowls.

To serve, pour the chilled gazpacho into a serving jug, place a bowl of crab and avocado in front of each guest and pour the gazpacho around the avocado and crab mound at the table. Drizzle with a few drops of olive oil and enjoy.

RIGHT: Jalapeno-infused gazpacho with avocado, blue swimmer crab and coriander

SERVING GAZPACHO

Gazpacho is served well chilled so it has to be well seasoned. Sherry vinegar gives it an acidic lift and the chilli is also important for balancing the flavour. The soup should sing with bright fresh flavours. The crab garnish should just be that—the soup is the main player. Give the soup a final whisking, just before serving to ensure it is well blended.

Crisp potato galette,

grilled goat's cheese, oven-dried tomatoes and herb salad

A feast of complementary flavours and textures make this galette a perfect vegetable entrée.

Ingredients

6–8 large potatoes (desirée or russet burbanks)

6 tablespoons Clarified butter (page 128)

Salad of herbs (page 139) or fresh chervil sprigs

200 g fresh goat's cheese, formed into 3 cm diameter logs

6 small Croûtons (page 134)

2 tablespoons whipped double cream

Olive oil

12 Oven-dried tomatoes (page 136)

2 tablespoons Red-wine vinaigrette (page 129)

1½ tablespoons Pistou (page 29)

Serves 6

To make the potato galettes, peel the potatoes and shape roughly into cylinders. Using a mandoline, slice the potato as finely as possibly into circles. On a lightly buttered non-stick flat tray, place a 14 cm diameter ring mould and place one potato slice in the centre of the mould and then layer and overlap the remaining potato slices around the edge, to form a disc. Repeat to form a second layer on top, placing one last potato slice in the centre. Brush lightly with the clarified butter and repeat to make another 5 galettes.

To cook the potato galettes, place the tray in a very hot preheated oven at 240°C for about 8–10 minutes until the galettes are golden brown on the bottom. Turn the galettes over when ready and cook on the second side for 4 minutes. Remove from the oven and set aside. The galettes can be prepared 1–2 hours ahead and reheated.

Prepare the herb salad.

Cut the goat's cheese logs into 3 cm-high discs and place onto a small croûton of bread (this prevents the cheese melting on the hot tray when it's under the grill). Spread a little of the cream evenly over the top of the goat's cheese and place on a tray under a hot grill until the top begins to blister and turn a glazed, golden brown. Remove the tray to a medium hot oven (180°C) to finish cooking.

Meanwhile, oil a flat tray and place the oven-dried tomatoes (cut in half lengthwise) on the tray skin down. Place in the oven to reheat. Reheat the potato galettes in the oven at the same time.

To serve, toss the herb salad with the vinaigrette and form 6 small piles of salad. When the galettes are hot, remove from the oven but leave them on the hot tray. Place a piece of goat's cheese in the centre of each galette and suround with the warmed tomatoes. Place this on warm plates and top the cheese with some salad of herbs and drizzle with a little pistou.

See photo page 138

or
pa

JOHN CHAPMAN

n Antwerp city centre. And
ed up 25 miles to the south
irport.

udgeon, an occupational
ked if anything could be
needed to be in London that
important hospital meeting.

ort staff shook their heads
sympathetically.

Her Antwerp flight left in
45 minutes. Even a fast taxi
would not get her there in
time. And her low-cost flight
ticket from Antwerp was non-
transferable.

A new ticket would cost
£90, which she could not
afford.

She was close to tears,
Then one of the airport staff
frantically gestured to her to
follow him.

Simultaneously, a voice
boomed over the tannoy.
"Miss Dudgeon, please proceed to gate 52."

Empty

Waiting at gate 52 was an
airline pilot and to her amaze-
ment he led her down a ramp
n to an empty Boeing 737.

Then, as the engines roared
life a voice over the
oy said: "Good after-
lady passenger. This is
aptain speaking.

will be in the air for
nutes before landing
p Airport."

Dudgeon was in
e to catch her
ound flight.

geon, of Clapham,
don, said: "I
ieve it. I had the
ane to myself.

Should your child be playing with the family pets this morning?

by SALLY STAPLES

FRIENDS of mine, who seem not to relish the quiet life, have recently acquired a labrador puppy in addition to their two young children and three cats.

I was invited over to lunch to meet the new arrival and fell for his roly-poly golden charm as did my small daughter who regarded both puppy and cats as prospective playmates.

But much to my friends surprise I didn't share their enthusiasm for children and animals rolling hysterically on the floor in horseplay.

"Oh but the puppy's so gentle. He wouldn't hurt a fly," I was told. "And the cats? Well they've grown up with the children. They'll put up with anything."

A situation like this is not easy. As fast as I whisked my daughter away from the playful cats' claws, the louder she clamoured to be allowed to run after them. The other children could play with the animals. Why couldn't she?

My friends, while highly intelligent on most matters, seemed to have a blind spot on this one. They couldn't or wouldn't accept that all animals have a natural instinct to defend themselves from children's provocative behaviour.

It takes only a second for a little finger to be jabbed into a cat's eye.

BISCUIT

The cat will not reason to itself: "That child doesn't know any better. It didn't mean to hurt me. I really must control my instinct to strike back." Instead the cat will lash out in self-defence and it only takes a second for a child to be blinded.

Last week a 19-month-old girl had her nose bitten off by an alsatian which playfully tried to snatch a biscuit that was half-hanging out of her mouth. More tragic still was the death of a seven-year-old little boy who was savaged to death by a boxer dog.

Accidents like these fill people with fear that an animal could attack their child. How on earth can it be prevented? The animals are often not naturally vicious but are provoked by children who do not realise what they are doing.

Surely the only answer is to train children, from the moment they can understand, that animals can be dangerous and should never be approached without caution and respect, that sudden movements and teasing are not allowed.

Some people tell me it is terrible to frighten children in this way. But with most lively toddlers it is often the only way to try and ensure their safety.

It is a remarkable fact that many animals put up with appalling abuse from children and tolerate their tails being yanked and fur pulled in a marvellously heroic way. Sometimes it is short-tempered parents who lash out more quickly than domestic pets.

But we should never forget that animals, however intelligent and affectionate, are not human beings. Their instinct is stronger than their reason. And so should ours be when it comes to protecting our young.

Summer pea and zucchini risotto

Risotto is usually eaten as an entrée in Italy but it can also serve as a main course when accompanied by a salad. All the whys, hows and whens of making risotto have been explained in many books—the following is a simple explanation to guide you through one of the great, classic Italian dishes.

Ingredients

60 g unsalted butter, chilled

1 small onion, peeled, finely chopped

1 cup arborio or carnaroli rice

¾ cup white wine

5 cups Chicken stock (page 131), simmering as needed

6 small zucchinis, flowers attached if possible, sliced

1 cup green peas, shelled, blanched, refreshed

3 tablespoons chopped fresh flat-leaf parsley

¼ cup grated parmesan cheese + extra

25 g butter

Sea salt and freshly ground black pepper

Serves 6–8

To prepare the risotto, melt the butter in a large heavy-bottomed saucepan over a medium low heat. Stir in the onions and sweat gently until softened and translucent, but without colouring, about 2–3 minutes. Add the rice and stir thoroughly with the butter and onions without colouring, about 3 minutes. Add the wine and bring to a simmer and stir until the wine has been absorbed. Keep stirring the rice to prevent it from sticking and increase the heat to medium. Add ½ cup of stock and continue stirring. It is best to have the simmering saucepan of stock next to the risotto saucepan on the stove. The rice will release its starch and the mixture should be starting to look creamy. Keep adding stock in ½ cup quantities to just cover the rice and keep stirring to maintain a creamy consistency. Repeat as the rice absorbs the stock. After 1 ½ cups of stock have been added, stir in the sliced zucchini and continue stirring and adding stock, until nearly all the stock has been used. Taste the rice from time to time to determine how cooked it is. Just before you think the rice is ready, add the peas and parsley to give them time to warm through. The finished rice should be cooked, but with a slight bite to it, not chalky, but not mushy either. When the rice is cooked (there may be stock left over but that's better than being caught short), the risotto should look moist but not runny.

To serve, quickly remove the risotto from the heat and stir in the cheese. Add the butter and stir vigorously to blend it and to bring the risotto together. Taste for seasoning and spoon into hot bowls. Extra parmesan can be served separately.

See photo page 130

Salad of kipfler potatoes, borlotti beans,
green beans and tomato

I love fresh borlotti beans. They have an unusual chalky texture and once you have acquired a taste for them you will find yourself putting them in dishes to add substance. Their beautiful, light purple colour when cooked, contrasts nicely in this salad of complementary flavours and textures.

Ingredients

Kipfler potato salad (page 60)

500 g fresh borlotti beans

1 cup Chickpeas, cooked (page 63)

200 g green runner beans, blanched, refreshed, sliced

6 egg-shaped (roma) tomatoes, peeled, seeded, cut into petals

6 spring onions, sliced finely

1 Roasted red capsicum (page 137), thin strips

3 tablespoons fresh flat-leaf parsley leaves, picked

2 tablespoons small fresh basil leaves

Sea salt and freshly ground black pepper

1 cup Lemon vinaigrette (page 129)

1 cup white fronds of curly endive, optional

Serves 6

To prepare the Kipfler potato salad, follow the instructions on page 60.

To prepare the fresh borlotti beans, shell them, place in a stainless steel saucepan and cover well with cold water. Bring to the boil, lower the heat and simmer until tender. Undercooked fresh, shelled beans are as bad as overcooked mushy beans, so begin checking the beans for tenderness after 10 minutes of simmering and test every minute from then on. Strain, and drain the beans and reserve.

To serve, place the potato salad on serving plates or one large platter. Place all the other ingredients in a large bowl, season and toss together with the vinaigrette. Place the contents of the bowl over the potatoes interlaying the textures and colours. Drizzle with more vinaigrette if needed and season. Toss in some white fronds of curly endive to lighten the salad if desired.

LEFT: Salad of kipfler potatoes, borlotti beans green beans and tomato

RIGHT: Polenta with grilled mushrooms, shaved parmesan and rocket (recipe overleaf)

Polenta with grilled mushrooms,
shaved parmesan and rocket

Unlimited variations of this dish can be created with other complementary ingredients such as young leeks, asparagus or broad beans. A few drops of white truffle oil will also enhance the flavour.

Ingredients

12 large field or flat-top mushrooms

3 tablespoons Clarified butter (page 128)

1 tablespoon minced garlic

Sea salt and freshly ground black pepper

2 tablespoons chopped fresh thyme leaves

6–12 wedges of Polenta (page 133)

½ cup extra-virgin olive oil

1 tablespoon balsamic vinegar

Shaved parmesan cheese

1 cup rocket leaves, stems removed

1 lemon, cut in wedges

Serves 6

To cook, preheat the grill. Brush the mushrooms with some of the clarified butter and garlic, season with salt, pepper and thyme, and brush again with clarified butter. Oil the hot plate and place the mushrooms and polenta wedges on the grill to cook at the same time. Turn the mushrooms and polenta as needed until the mushrooms are tender and the polenta is golden or marked by the grill and warmed through.

To serve, place the polenta onto warm plates, top with the mushrooms and drizzle with extra virgin olive oil and balsamic vinegar. Top with the shaved Parmesan and rocket and drizzle over a little more olive oil and balsamic. Serve with the lemon wedges and grind black pepper over everything.

Grilled salad of roasted capsicums,
anchovies and basil

Grilling capsicums after they have been roasted adds an extra dimension to their flavour. Especially when tossed with fresh basil while they are still warm.

Ingredients

3 Roasted red capsicums (page 137), skins removed

3 roasted yellow capsicums, skins removed

1 cup extra-virgin olive oil

½ cup basil leaves, torn

1 teaspoon minced garlic

Sea salt and freshly ground black pepper

24 good quality anchovy fillets

½ cup small black olives

2 tablespoons balsamic vinegar

Serves 6

To prepare the capsicums, preheat a ridged grill plate over high heat. Separate the capsicums, into their natural lobes and dry them well on absorbent paper.

Paint the grill with a little olive oil. When it sizzles, lay the capsicums along the grill, skin side down first and leave until the capsicums are marked with lines, about 1 minute. Working quickly with tongs, turn the capsicums to right angles and continue grilling for 1 minute. Remove from the grill and place on a tray in a single layer. Immediately sprinkle with half the torn basil leaves and garlic and drizzle well with extra-virgin olive oil. Season with black pepper and leave to marinate and cool.

To serve the capsicums, arrange them on a large platter in a decorative pattern, alternating the colours. Add the anchovy fillets, black olives, the remaining fresh basil leaves, the marinating juices and oil and sprinkle a little balsamic vinegar over. Taste for salt and season if needed.

Salad of roasted beetroot, asparagus,
lamb's lettuce and goat's cheese

A refreshing salad of early summer vegetables and goat's cheese. Roasting the beetroot concentrates its depth of flavour.

Ingredients

3 beetroot

3 tablespoons walnut oil

3 tablespoons extra-virgin olive oil

1½ tablespoons red-wine vinegar

Sea salt and freshly ground black pepper

16 asparagus stalks, peeled

½ cup lamb's lettuce (mâche) or watercress

½ cup curly endive, white part only

2 tablespoons pine nuts, toasted

150 g fresh goat's cheese

1 tablespoon fresh chervil sprigs

½ tablespoon snipped fresh chives

Serves 4

To bake the beetroot, preheat the oven to 190°C. Wash the beetroot if necessary and trim off the tops. Place them on a baking tray and roast in the oven for 40–60 minutes. It takes a while to roast, but should be ready when it can be pierced easily with a knife and has collapsed quite a bit. Remove and allow to cool a little—the skin should slip off readily. Cut the beetroot into wedges.

To prepare vinaigrette, mix together in a bowl the walnut oil, olive oil and vinegar with salt and pepper. Dress the beetroot with the vinaigrette and set aside.

Cook the asparagus in plenty of boiling salted water for about 3 minutes. Remove and drain well, season and toss with a little vinaigrette.

To serve, toss the salads (lamb's lettuce and curly endive) in vinaigrette. Place the beetroot wedges in the centre of four plates and top with the salads. Arrange the asparagus around the salads and sprinkle over the pine nuts. Slice the goat's cheese and place on the salad and sprinkle with the herbs. Spoon a little of the beetroot juice around the plates along with some vinaigrette and grind some black pepper over.

The great outdoors

Everyday dinners

One of the delights of summer is outdoor eating. We tend to feel more alive eating outdoors and yet more at ease. A sense of lingering pervades as you relax. Hopefully the large variety of recipes in this chapter will entice you to enjoy more of these leisurely occasions.

Some of the recipes, such as the Veal escalopes with herbs and lemon and the John Dory with spinach and pine nuts are easily prepared and cooked in a few minutes. A carefully made Potato salad is a great dish. It can be substantial, but used in small quantities as the base of lighter dishes such as the Grilled prawns and octopus or the Duck livers with figs, the balance always seems right. Whole chick peas appear in the Spicy stew with tomato and potato and again under the Swordfish with romesco sauce. I love chick peas in all their guises and their versatility is certainly fascinating.

Australians love lamb and trimmed rib-eye of lamb is possibly my favourite cut. It tastes like lamb, cooks quickly, and when kept pink in the centre and rested well, retains its succulence and flavour. It has a natural affinity with the Provençal-style vegetables served with it and combined with the Basil oil and black olive butter has a harmony of integrated flavours. The Paillard of lamb is thinly sliced and quickly cooked to secure the fresh intense flavours.

The chicken dishes offer another contrast and will hopefully encourage you to buy good quality whole chickens. Follow the recipe for Grilled chicken breast with eggplant, tomato and zucchini to use the breasts for the first meal. The following day use the legs in the Chicken legs with green olives, preserved lemon and coriander. It will make an interesting change—two quite different flavour spectrums and varying cooking techniques.

Slow-cooked veal shanks with potato gnocchi, mushrooms and peas is exactly the type of dish I love the most. It's full of complex, satisfying tastes and aromas developed by the long slow cooking. Careful braising transforms tough cuts of meat into meltingly soft dishes with great depth of flavour. Removing the veal from the bone after it has braised and shredding it into smaller pieces gives the dish a lighter balance for summer.

RIGHT: Grilled prawns and octopus on kipfler potatoes with tomato herb vinaigrette (recipe overleaf)

Grilled prawns and octopus
on kipfler potatoes with tomato herb vinaigrette

A carefully prepared potato salad is a wonderful dish. The secret is to use good waxy potatoes (I like kipflers the best) and to dress the potatoes while they are still hot so they can absorb all the flavours. The technique below keeps the potatoes from becoming a crumbling mess.

Ingredients

Kipfler potato salad

500 g kipfler or any waxy potatoes

2 tablespoons finely chopped golden shallots

2 tablespoons finely chopped green shallots

Sea salt and freshly ground black pepper

2 tablespoons chopped fresh flat-leaf parsley

5 tablespoons Lemon vinaigrette (page 129)

4 tablespoons snipped fresh chives

Tomato herb vinaigrette

4 ripe egg-shaped tomatoes (roma), peeled, seeded, diced, well drained

2 golden shallots, peeled, finely chopped

6 tablespoons Lemon vinaigrette (page 129)

2 tablespoons chopped fresh flat-leaf parsley

2 tablespoons snipped fresh basil leaves

10 coriander seeds, crushed

1 serrano or similar hot chilli, seeded, chopped

18 prawns, shelled, de-veined, washed

9 baby octopus, cleaned, halved

Olive oil

18 green beans, tipped, cooked, refreshed

Serves 6

To prepare the potato salad, gently boil the potatoes in salted water over a low heat (kipfler potatoes are fragile once they are cooked). Drain the potatoes when they are cooked and peel them while they are still hot.

Slice the potatoes in 1 cm rounds and place them on a flat tray with sides. Cover the tray with potatoes in a single layer and sprinkle them with the chopped golden shallots and green shallots. Season well with salt, pepper and parsley and spoon over the vinaigrette. Add the chives just before serving.

To prepare the tomato herb vinaigrette, mix all the ingredients and leave to marinate for 15 minutes for the flavour to develop.

To cook the seafood, preheat a grill until very hot. Season the prawns and octopus and oil the grill. Place the octopus and prawns on the grill and cook quickly turning as needed, about 2 minutes.

Meanwhile, begin serving. Carefully place the potato salad and some vinaigrette on a platter or plates and top with the green beans. Once the prawns and octopus are ready, remove from the grill and place on top of the potatoes and beans. Spoon over the tomato herb vinaigrette while it's all still hot.

CLEANING OCTOPUS AND DE-VEINING AND BUTTERFLYING PRAWNS
To clean the octopus, cut off their heads with a sharp knife and discard. Cut out the beak in the centre of each tentacle and discard. Wash the tentacles well. To de-vein the prawns, shell them and then run a knife down the length of the prawn and remove the black intestinal vein. Wash around this area well. To butterfly the prawns, cut deeper lengthwise into the flesh and then flatten out, that is, open them out to a butterfly-shape.

Spicy chickpea, potato and tomato stew

A summer vegetable stew hearty enough to provide a light dinner. I am very fond of chick peas—an ancient legume with a slightly, nutty flavour. They feature in salads, soups, stews, pastas, purées, fritters and crèpes throughout the Mediterranean, Middle East and India.

Ingredients

4 tablespoons olive oil

1 onion, finely chopped

2 teaspoons minced garlic

800 g potatoes, peeled, cut into 2 cm dice or quartered

2 carrots, peeled, sliced 5 mm thick

2 Roasted red capsicums (page 137), cut in 1 cm strips

2 cups Chick peas, cooked, (page 63)

1 teaspoon fresh thyme leaves

2 teaspoons fresh oregano leaves

3 teaspoons crushed cumin seeds

1 teaspoon dried red chilli, crushed

800–g tin egg-shaped (roma) tomatoes, coarsely chopped + juice

Sea salt and freshly ground black pepper

1½ cups water

2 tablespoons chopped parsley

Serves 8

To prepare the vegetable stew, heat the olive oil in a medium-sized saucepan over a low heat and sweat the onion, with the lid on, to soften. Remove the lid and allow to colour a little. Add the garlic and stir for 30–60 seconds to soften. Add the potatoes, carrots, red capsicums, chick peas, thyme, oregano, cumin, chilli, chopped tomatoes and the tomato juice, salt and pepper. Bring to the boil over a medium heat. Add the water, up to 1½ cups to moisten the stew. There is no need to add all the water if a lot of juices have collected. Bring to the boil, turn the heat to low, cover and simmer slowly for about 30 minutes. Check the potatoes are tender and correct the seasoning.

To serve, spoon the stew into deep bowls, sprinkle with parsley and serve with crusty bread.

Grilled swordfish with chick peas,
artichoke hearts, leeks and romesco vinaigrette

Swordfish cut into even-sized steaks is perfect for grilling and robust enough to marry well with a large range of Mediterranean flavours. Romesco is a Catalan speciality, a mildly hot sauce used widely to enhance many dishes.

Ingredients

150 g chick peas

Romesco sauce

2 ripe egg-shaped (roma) tomatoes, cored

2 red capsicums, roasted (page 137)

3 cloves garlic, roasted (page 91)

2 tablespoons blanched almonds, lightly dry roasted

4 dried red chillies

3 tablespoons white-wine vinegar

1⅕ cups extra-virgin olive oil

Sea salt and freshly ground black pepper

Continued overleaf

Cover the chick peas generously with water and soak overnight in the refrigerator.

To make the romesco sauce, preheat the oven to 200°C. Place the tomatoes on an oiled tray and roast in the oven for 15–20 minutes—they should be soft. Reserve and when they have cooled, peel them, chop coarsely and save all the juices. Chop the capsicums and garlic coarsely and put in the food processor along with the tomato mixture. Chop the almonds and chillies and add to the tomato mixture. Pulse to blend the mixture in a food processor while adding the vinegar to blend. Pour the olive oil in a stream and season to taste. Keep refrigerated in an airtight container if not using immediately—it will keep for 3–4 days.

To cook the chick peas, drain the soaked chick peas, which will have doubled in size, rinse, and place
Continued overleaf

LEFT: Grilled swordfish with chick peas, artichoke hearts, leeks and romesco vinaigrette

RIGHT: John Dory fillet with spinach, preserved lemon and pine nuts (overleaf)

1 bay leaf

3 fresh thyme sprigs

1 onion, peeled

9 artichoke hearts, good quality, preserved in olive oil,
     drained and halved

12 young leeks, blanched and refreshed

Sea salt and freshly ground black pepper

¾ cup Lemon vinaigrette (page 129)

6 180-g swordfish steaks, each 2 cm thick

Olive oil

1 red serrano or similar hot chilli, seeded, chopped

1 lemon, cut into wedges

Serves 6

SALTING DRIED PULSES
Add salt towards the end of
cooking dried beans, lentils
and any other pulses as the
salt prolongs the cooking
time of the beans.

them in a large saucepan. Cover well with cold water and add the bay leaf, thyme sprigs and onion but don't salt. Bring to the boil, lower the heat and simmer gently for 1½ hours, testing after 1 hour. Add salt near the finish of cooking. Drain the chick peas once they are cooked— they should be soft but retain their shape—and tip out into a flat container to cool, covered with a wet tea towel. Once cooled, rub off the skin of the chick peas.

To cook the swordfish, preheat the grill over a high heat and brush the grill with olive oil. Season the swordfish with black pepper and grill on the first side to a light golden colour, about 2 minutes. Turn the fish over and complete the cooking, keeping the swordfish moist in the centre. Remove the swordfish to a warm tray to rest for a minute.

Meanwhile, place the chick peas, artichokes and young leeks in a steamer and reheat quickly. Turn into a bowl, season well and spoon in 3 tablespoons of romesco sauce to lightly coat the vegetables. Distribute the vegetables evenly onto the centre of each plate and spoon around a little lemon vinaigrette and more romesco sauce.

To serve, place the swordfish, and any juices left on the tray, over the warmed vegetables. Top the swordfish with the chopped chilli, drizzle with lemon vinaigrette and sprinkle with sea salt. Serve with lemon wedges.

John Dory fillet with spinach,
preserved lemon and pine nuts

Always popular, John Dory must be cooked carefully to be at its best. It's delicious with this typical Silician-style garnish.

Ingredients

6 150-g John Dory fillets, skin on

4 tablespoons Clarified butter (page 128)

Sea salt and freshly ground black pepper

1 bunch spinach, leaves picked, washed well

3 tablespoons sultanas, soaked in water, drained

3 tablespoons pine nuts, dry roasted

3 tablespoons diced Preserved lemons (page 39)

2 tablespoons small black olives, stoned and sliced

Continued on next page

To prepare the John Dory, make 1 or 2 slashes in the skin of the fish with the tip of a sharp knife. Thoroughly dry the skin by pressing down on it with the back of a large knife and drawing it along the fillet and wiping each time with a dry cloth. This will help the skin to crisp evenly and quickly.

To cook the fish, melt the clarified butter in 2 teflon-coated frying pans over a high heat. Lightly season the John Dory fillets and place in the pans skin side down. Press down on the fish with a metal spatula to

¾ cup Lemon vinaigrette (page 129)

About 2 tablespoons grated parmesan cheese

1 lemon, cut into 6 wedges

Serves 6

keep it flat and cook until the skin is a golden colour, about 2 minutes. Lower the heat, turn the fish over and complete the cooking for 1 minute. The fish will just about be cooked on the first side and only need minimal cooking on the second side, so watch it carefully.

Meanwhile, cook the spinach in a large pot of boiling salted water until just cooked and wilted, about 1 minute. Drain well in a colander, pressing down on the spinach to extract excess moisture, and wrap up quickly in a clean tea towel. Then place it into a warm bowl and add the sultanas, pine nuts, preserved lemon and olives. Season well while mixing all the ingredients together with a little lemon vinaigrette.

To serve, spoon the spinach mixture onto the centre of warm plates and sprinkle each with grated parmesan. Remove the fish from the pans and place on the spinach. Drizzle more lemon vinaigrette over the fish and plate, sprinkle with sea salt and serve with the lemon wedges.

Spanish potato and onion tortilla

Of all the tortilla and frittata variations I have tried I still like this one the best. Perhaps it's the simplicity of the ingredients that always seem so satisfying.

Ingredients

2 tablespoons olive oil + ½ cup extra

1 onion, peeled, finely sliced

1 kg desiree or similiar potato, peeled and cut in 3 cm dice

Sea salt and freshly ground black pepper

1 teaspoon chopped fresh rosemary

6 eggs

3 tablespoons chopped fresh flat-leaf parsley

4 tablespoons olive oil

Serves 4

To prepare the tortilla, place the 2 tablespoons of olive oil in a large frying pan over a medium heat and add the onion. Sauté until the onion is lightly golden and well wilted. Drain the onions through a sieve and set aside. Add half a cup of olive oil to the pan and return to a medium heat. Add the potato, season with a little salt and the rosemary and sauté, stirring frequently. Don't be in too much of a hurry—allow the potatoes to cook through and become lightly golden on the sides. Check that they are cooked by cutting a few in half—they should not be opaque in the centre. Drain in the sieve over the onions. Break the eggs into a mixing bowl, add the chopped parsley and season well with salt and pepper. Mix lightly together.

To cook the tortilla, place a 25 cm diameter Teflon frying pan over a medium heat and add 4 tablespoons of olive oil. Pour in the egg mixture and add the potatoes and onions pressing down and moving them around so they fit evenly in the pan. Turn the heat to low, cover the pan and cook gently until they are golden on the bottom, about 8–10 minutes. Invert the tortilla onto a plate or flat tray, slide it back into the pan and cook until it is set, about 6–8 minutes. Slide onto a flat platter and serve it into wedges, warm or at room temperature, accompanied by crusty bread.

Grilled duck livers and figs
with kipfler potatoes

A quickly cooked grill. The richness of the duck livers is balanced by the sweetness of the grilled figs and lifted by the balsamic vinegar.

Ingredients
Shallot and balsamic vinegar sauce

1 teaspoon very finely chopped golden shallots

½ teaspoon chopped fresh thyme leaves

6 fresh rosemary leaves, chopped

½ cup reduced veal stock (page 132), warm

2½ tablespoons extra-virgin olive oil

3 teaspoons balsamic vinegar

Sea salt and freshly ground black pepper

Kipfler potato salad (page 60)

6 lamb's lettuce (mâche) or curly endive, washed

½ cup picked watercress sprigs

2 tablespoons snipped fresh chives

6 ripe figs, cut in half across

12–18 duck livers, depending on size, trimmed of fibre and green bile spots

Serves 6

To make the sauce, place the shallots, thyme and rosemary in a small bowl and mix together. Pour in the warm veal stock, then the olive oil and balsamic vinegar but do not whisk them together to emulsify them. Gently stir the sauce with a spoon and season to taste, the sauce should have a kick from the vinegar. Reserve in a warm place. Prepare the potato salad, salad leaves and chives.

To cook the figs, preheat a grill to hot. Place the cut side of the figs onto the grill top to sear, turn over and continue grilling for 1–2 minutes. The figs should be well warmed through without completely collapsing.

Meanwhile, grill the livers quickly on all sides keeping them pink in the centre, about 2–3 minutes. Remove the livers and figs and keep warm.

To serve, place the potato salad on each plate or bowl and top with the livers. Place the figs on top of the livers and spoon over the shallot and balsamic sauce to moisten well. Sprinkle with chives and place some salad on top of the figs.

RIGHT: Grilled quails on cavolo nero, pine nuts, lemon and thyme (recipe overleaf)

FAR RIGHT: Grilled duck livers and figs with kipfler potatoes

Grilled quails on cavolo nero,
pine nuts, lemon and thyme

The secret of this dish is in the sauce—a blend of veal stock, butter and quail juices lifted by the lemon and thyme.

Ingredients

12 quails, butterflied, boned (page 80)

4 tablespoons olive oil + extra

Sea salt and freshly ground black pepper

2 tablespoons fresh thyme leaves + extra

2 tablespoons unsalted butter + extra

6 Polenta wedges (page 133), fried or grilled

½ cup reduced Veal stock (page 132)

3 tablespoons lemon juice, strained

2 bunches cavolo nero or 300 g spinach, picked and washed

3 tablespoons pine nuts, dry roasted

6 lemon wedges

Serves 6

To cook the quails, season them with olive oil, salt and pepper and sprinkle with thyme leaves. Carefully press some thyme inside the quails between the skin and flesh. Preheat the grill to hot and lay the quails skin side down onto the oiled grill. Seal well on this side first before turning. Moisten with a little more oil or butter. Grill or fry the polenta wedges at the same time.

Meanwhile, heat the veal stock and spoon onto an ovenproof tray. Add the lemon juice and butter and extra thyme. When the quails are almost cooked, place them on top of the sauce on the tray and finish in a hot preheated oven at 200°C for 2–3 minutes. At the same time cook the cavolo nero or spinach in plenty of boiling salted water for 2 minutes. Drain well and squeeze lightly to remove excess water.

To serve, butter and season the cavolo nero or spinach, add the pine nuts and lay down the centre of each warm plate. Place the hot polenta beside the cavolo nero or spinach and arrange the quails over both. Pour the quail juices and sauce, which have collected on the tray, over the quail. Serve with lemon wedges.

CAVOLO NERO

Cavolo nero is Italian black cabbage and resembles silverbeet more than spinach. When cooked, it retains some structure and slight resistence to the bite. It is usually picked quite young in Australia with small leaves and tender stems. This enables you to cook it as is. If the leaves are larger the centre stem will need to be removed. Europeans always pick cavolo nero after their first frost which naturally softens the toughened stems.

Grilled chicken breast
with eggplant, tomato and zucchini

It's worthwhile purchasing the best quality chicken—it does make a difference to the flavour of the dish and it will remind you how delicious chicken really is. This dish is a quick way to serve chicken with summer vegetables and herbs if you are prepared to do a little preparation beforehand.

Ingredients

½ **cup olive oil**

2 small Japanese eggplants, sliced in thin rounds

2 zucchinis, thinly sliced into rounds

1 tablespoon unsalted butter, softened

3 egg-shaped tomatoes, peeled, seeded, cut into strips

2 tablespoons fresh basil leaves, torn

2 teaspoons fresh tarragon leaves

¼ **cup Cherry tomato coulis (page 47)**

4 150–g chicken breasts, wing bone trimmed, skin on

Sea salt and freshly ground black pepper

Serves 4

To prepare the vegetables, heat 3 tablespoons of the olive oil in a large frying pan over a medium heat and add the eggplant slices. Fry until lightly browned on the first side, about 2 minutes, turn over and finish cooking on the second side, about 1 minute. Remove and drain on absorbent paper. Drain the oil from the pan and add another 3 tablespoons of olive oil, then add the zucchini slices. Cook until lightly browned on the first side, about 2 minutes. Turn over and finish cooking, about 1 minute. Lightly butter 4 dinner plates and arrange the eggplant, zucchini and tomato slices so they overlap each other around the outside of each plate. Sprinkle with a few of the torn basil leaves and all the tarragon leaves. Spoon some cherry tomato coulis in the centre of each plate and thinly paint a little coulis over the vegetables.

To cook the chicken, preheat a flat grill top or barbecue plate and brush with oil. Sprinkle the chicken breasts with salt and grill, skin side down for 3–4 minutes. Check the chicken and continue cooking for another 2–3 minutes if necessary. Turn the chicken over and grill until the chicken begins to feel firm, about 3 minutes. Remove from the grill to a warm flat tray, cover well and let it rest to finish cooking with its own heat.

To serve the chicken, warm the 4 prepared plates in a preheated oven at 180°C, for about 2–3 minutes. Remove the plates from the oven, cut the chicken once, diagonally, through the breast and arrange a breast in the centre of the vegetables on each warm plate. Pour any chicken juices left on the tray over the chicken and sprinkle with the remaining fresh basil leaves. Grind a little black pepper over the dish and serve immediately.

Rib eye of lamb,
Provençal-style vegetables and black-olive butter

LEFT: Rib eye of lamb,
Provençal-style vegetables
and black-olive butter

In this hearty dish the black-olive butter melts into the succulent lamb sitting on a bed of aromatic vegetables. Make it for special occasions but for mid-week meals keep a reserve of black-olive butter and basil oil to flavour quickly grilled meat and vegetables.

Ingredients

Basil oil

1 cup firmly packed fresh basil leaves

1 cup extra-virgin olive oil

Black-olive butter

4 tablespoons finely chopped golden shallots

500 g unsalted butter, softened

38 black olives, stoned and chopped

2 tablespoons Dijon mustard

1½ tablespoons strained lemon juice

5 tablespoons Tapenade (page 32)

Sea salt and freshly ground black pepper

Provençal-style vegetables

500 g small elongated eggplant

500 g zucchini

3 red capsicums, roasted and peeled (page 137)

Extra-virgin olive oil

3 fresh thyme branches

2 onions, cut in half and thinly sliced

2 teaspoons minced garlic

500 g egg-shaped (roma) tomatoes, peeled, seeded, diced

16 fresh basil leaves

Sea salt and freshly ground black pepper

Freshly ground coriander seed

10 black olives, stoned and coarsely chopped

4 teaspoons tiny capers, rinsed

5 teaspoons sherry vinegar

8 lamb rib-eye fillets, trimmed of fat and sinew

3 teaspoons balsamic vinegar

Serves 8

To make the basil oil, bring a small saucepan of water to the boil and blanch the basil leaves for 30 seconds. Remove the basil with a slotted spoon and when cool, squeeze out as much liquid as possible. In a blender, combine the basil and the oil and purée for 2–3 minutes until the basil is finely chopped. Let stand 2–3 hours, then strain through a double layer of cheesecloth into a clean jar. Cover and refrigerate until needed.

To make the black-olive butter, sweat the shallots in a little butter to soften. Place the remaining butter in a food processor or blender and whisk until white. Add the remaining ingredients and blend together until completely smooth. Remove the butter and roll it into logs 3–4 cm in diameter. Cover securely with foil and store in the refrigerator.

To make the Provençal-style vegetables, cut each eggplant lengthwise into 6 pieces. Then cut the lengths into 1 cm cubes. Top and tail the zucchini and cut lengthwise into strips 5 mm wide, keeping the skin attached to the strips. Then cut in half to form batons 1 cm x 3 cm. Cut the capsicums into 2 cm x 6 cm strips or the length of the capsicums.

Pour some olive oil into a large frying pan and heat to very hot. Add the eggplant and 1 branch of thyme and cook until well done, tossing and stirring as needed. Drain in a colander set over a bowl and set aside. Repeat the process for the zucchini.

Sweat the onions in some olive oil in a frying pan over a medium-low heat until they soften and slightly colour. Add the garlic and cook another minute. Add the tomato dice and continue to cook down until slightly
Continued overleaf

blended but some tomato dice is still showing. Add the capsicums to the mix and season with 1 branch thyme, basil, salt, pepper and coriander and cook for 1–2 minutes. Mix the eggplant and zucchini with the tomato, capsicums, onion mixture and stir to blend together. Add the black olives, capers and sherry vinegar and cover the pan with a lid. Place in a preheated oven at 150°C for 5 minutes to meld the flavours. Remove and keep warm, or allow to cool and serve at room temperature.

To cook the lamb, season with salt and pepper and brown it well on all sides in a hot frying pan, about 2 minutes. Place the lamb on a rack over a pan and finish cooking in the hot oven for 7–8 minutes for pink lamb. Remove and leave in a warm place to rest for 10 minutes.

To serve, place some Provençal vegetables in the centre of each plate. Arrange to show off the colours and ingredients. Paint with a little basil oil to make the vegetables shine. Pour more basil oil close to the vegetables around the pile and add a little balsamic vinegar. Slice the lamb in half lengthwise and place, overlapping, on the vegetables. Top with a generous slice of black-olive butter and serve.

Paillard of lamb loin
with summer beans, tomato and tapenade

A quick and easy dish when you have the basic ingredients on hand. A paillard is a thin slice of lamb, cooked quickly so it stays moist.

Ingredients

6 lamb loins, trimmed of fat and silver skin

1 cup Tomato sauce (page 136)

300 g baby green beans, topped

Sea salt and freshly ground black pepper

3 tablespoons butter

3 tablespoons olive oil

1 tablespoon Lamb spice mix (page 88)

2 tablespoons tapenade

¼ cup extra-virgin olive oil

1 tablespoon balsamic vinegar

To prepare the lamb, place it on a cutting board and butterfly it by slicing the loin horizontally—but not all the way through. Open it out and flatten it gently with the bottom of a heavy saucepan so it is uniformly 1 cm thick.

To prepare the garnishes, heat the tomato sauce over a medium-low heat and keep warm. Cook the beans until tender in a large pot of boiling salted water, about 3 minutes. Drain, season, butter them well and keep warm.

To cook the lamb, preheat the grill until it is very hot and brush with the olive oil. Sprinkle each lamb loin with a little of the spice mix and place on the grill and cook for 1 minute. Turn the meat over and cook for 1 minute—the lamb will be pink. Reserve and season.

To serve, distribute the beans on warm plates and top with the tomato sauce. Spread each lamb loin with a layer of tapenade and place on top of the tomato. Pour the extra-virgin olive oil and balsamic vinegar over each lamb loin and serve. immediately.

Chicken with green olives,
preserved lemon and coriander

A lively summer, chicken dish based on a Moroccan-style blend of ingredients.

Ingredients

Broth

2 tablespoons olive oil

½ onion, finely chopped

2 teaspoons minced garlic

2 teaspoons grated fresh ginger

Bunch fresh coriander roots, well washed, chopped

¼ teaspoon ground cinnamon

½ teaspoon saffron threads, soaked in ¼ cup warm water

2 cups chicken stock (page 131)

4 chicken legs, cut into thighs and lower legs, trimmed

Sea salt and freshly ground black pepper

½ cup olive oil

3 tablespoons pitted and coarsely chopped green olives

1½ tablespoons diced Preserved lemon (page 39)

½ carrot, julienned, blanched, refreshed

2 tablespoons fresh coriander leaves (from bunch above)

Serves 4

To prepare the broth, place the olive oil in a heavy-bottomed saucepan over a low heat. Add the onion and sweat for 3 minutes. Add garlic, ginger, coriander roots, cinnamon and saffron with its water and cook for 2 minutes. Increase the heat to high and add the chicken stock, boil and then simmer for 20 minutes or until it is reduced to 2 cups of stock. Strain the broth and set aside.

To prepare the chicken, preheat the oven to 200°C. Season the chicken with salt and pepper. Heat the olive oil in an oven-proof frying pan over a medium-high heat, add the chicken and fry, turning occasionally until golden brown all over, about 8–10 minutes. Add half the prepared broth and place the pan in the oven to finish cooking for about 40–50 minutes. The chicken should be well cooked right through to the bone. Remove the chicken from the oven and keep warm.

To finish the sauce and chicken, reheat the remaining broth in a separate saucepan over a medium heat. Add the olives, preserved lemon, carrot and season with pepper and check if more salt is needed. Add the chicken pieces and any juices in the pan and cook for 1 minute to combine all the ingredients. Sprinkle with coriander leaves, mixing these in at the last moment. Place the chicken on warm plates and spoon over the sauce.

Serve with warm couscous if desired.

Potato gnocchi
with slow-cooked veal shanks, mushrooms and peas

Not every summer's day is glorious, so cook this dish on a cooler night to warm you through. This is a light way of cooking veal shanks.

Ingredients

Veal shanks

6 young veal shanks, tipped and trimmed

6 tablespoons olive oil

4 tablespoons flour

½ cup white wine

6 cups veal stock

2 tablespoons tomato paste

1 onion, peeled, sliced

2 celery stalks, cut in 3 cm lengths

2 carrots, peeled, sliced in 2 cm lengths

1 bouquet garni (thyme, parsley, bay leaves, peppercorns)

1 garlic bulb, halved horizontally

1 tablespoon fresh thyme leaves

Potato gnocchi

750 g binjte or desiree potatoes, washed

125–150 g flour + extra

1 60-g egg

50 g parmesan cheese

Sea salt and freshly ground black pepper

12 portobello or Swiss brown mushrooms, trimmed

6 tablespoons green peas, shelled, blanched, and refreshed

1 tablespoon chopped fresh thyme leaves

2 tablespoons chopped fresh parsley

Serves 6

RIGHT: Potato gnocchi with slow-cooked veal shanks, mushrooms and peas

To make the veals shanks, preheat the oven to 160°C. Trim the veals shanks by cutting around the bone to remove the membranes. This prevents the meat from clinging to the top of the bone while cooking. Heat 4 tablespoons of oil over a high flame in a large heavy-bottomed frying pan. Dust the shanks with flour, then seal them on all sides in the pan until browned. Remove the shanks and reserve to drain.

Pour away any remaining oil from the pan and deglaze it with the white wine over a high heat. Reduce over a high flame and add the veal stock and tomato paste. Bring to the boil.

Meanwhile in another frying pan, heat the remaining oil and cook the onion, celery and carrots until they begin to brown. Place the shanks in a braising dish just large enough to contain the shanks. Surround the shanks with the vegetables, bouquet garni and garlic halves. Pour over the hot veal stock and bring back to a near boil. Cover and place in the preheated oven to braise for 2–3 hours depending on the size of the shanks. The meat should be very soft and falling off the bone. Remove the shanks from the dish and set aside to cool. Strain the stock through a fine sieve, discard the vegetables and leave to settle for 5 minutes. Spoon off any fat from the top of the stock. Pour the stock into a clean saucepan and reduce by half.

Once the shanks are cool enough to handle, remove the meat from the bones and place in the reduced stock. Using two forks, shred the meat into small pieces in the sauce, add some thyme and set aside or refrigerate until ready to serve.

To make the potato gnocchi, preheat the oven to 175°C. Bake the potatoes for 1 hour or until well cooked. Split the potatoes, scoop out the flesh and press through a sieve or mash. Place the potatoes in a large bowl, fold in the flour and then gently add the egg, parmesan, salt and pepper, being careful not to overwork the dough. *Continued overleaf*

To prepare the gnocchi, roll the dough into a 2 cm cylinder on a lightly floured bench. Cut into 1–2 cm pieces and roll the pieces over a gnocchi paddle or the back of a fork to mark a groove. Place small batches of gnocchi in a large saucepan of boiling water and as the gnocchi rises to the surface remove them with a sieve. Place the cooked gnocchi in a warm bowl while you cook the rest.

Meanwhile, place the mushrooms on a well buttered tray, season them and roast in the already hot oven until cooked, about 10–15 minutes. At the same time reheat the veal shanks in their sauce, adding the peas, thyme and half the parsley towards the end to heat through.

To serve, add the warm gnocchi to the veal shank mixture and heat together quickly for 1 minute. Cut the mushrooms into small wedges and place in the serving bowls. Spoon over the gnocchi and shanks and sprinkle with the remaining parsley.

Veal escalopes with herbs and lemon

The secret to veal escalopes or scaloppini is to keep it simple. Cook the veal quickly and deglaze the pan with white wine and lemon juice. Serve with a shaved fennel and cos salad dressed with lemon vinaigrette or rice pilaf and marinated artichokes.

Ingredients

1 tablespoon chopped fresh tarragon

3 tablespoons chopped fresh chervil

8 veal escalopes, beaten thin between cling-wrap

⅓ cup of olive oil

Sea salt and freshly ground black pepper

⅓ cup dry white wine

2 tablespoons fresh lemon juice

50 g butter, chilled, diced

Serves 4

To prepare the veal escalopes, place the fresh herbs on a flat plate. Paint the veal escalopes lightly with olive oil on one side only. Place the oiled side of an escalope onto the herbs, pressing down lightly so the herbs stick to the veal. Remove the veal, herb-side up to a flat tray and repeat with the remaining veal. Reserve for 10 minutes.

To cook the veal, have everything ready, as it takes no time at all to finish the dish. Heat 1 or 2 large frying pans over a high heat and brush each pan with a little olive oil. Season the veal lightly with salt and pepper. Place the veal in the pan herb-side down and cook for 2 minutes. Turn the veal over and cook for 1 minute. Remove the veal escalopes, place on a tray and keep in a warm place. Meanwhile, deglaze the pan with the white wine and lemon juice over a high heat. Scrape the pan to release any bits on the bottom and reduce the liquid to a light syrup. Remove from the heat, add the butter and swirl the pan to incorporate the butter into the sauce.

To serve, place the veal onto 4 warm plates, spoon over the sauce and serve at once.

Spaghetti with mushrooms,
garlic, asparagus and chervil

A favourite combination of early summer vegetables tossed with spaghetti—a dish that heralds in summer and lighter meals.

Ingredients

400 g spaghetti

Sea salt and freshly ground black pepper

2½ tablespoons extra-virgin olive oil

50 g unsalted butter

200 g Swiss brown mushrooms, quartered

2 teaspoons minced garlic

18 asparagus spears, peeled, blanched, refreshed, diced

½ cup green peas, blanched, refreshed

1 tablespoon finely sliced green shallots

1 teaspoon red jalapeno or similar medium-hot chilli, seeded, finely chopped

2 tablespoons chopped fresh chervil

2 teaspoons Vinaigrette (page 129)

½ cup finely grated parmesan cheese

Serves 6

To cook the spaghetti, place it in a saucepan of at least 5 litres of boiling salted water. Cook at a rapid boil until al dente, about 7–8 minutes, or according to the packet instructions. Drain, but always leave a few tablespoons of the cooking water with the pasta to help it integrate with the sauce and garnish.

Meanwhile, have another saucepan of boiling salted water ready, siting over a high heat, so you can quickly reheat the asparagus, peas and green shallots. Keep a strainer ready on the side.

At the same time, melt the extra-virgin olive oil and half the butter in a large frying pan over a high heat and sauté the mushrooms with the garlic until well cooked. Add the reheated and drained asparagus, peas and green shallots to the mushrooms and season well. Tip the contents of this pan into a large stainless steel bowl and place over the saucepan of hot water to keep warm.

To serve, add the pasta to the bowl, along with the chilli, chervil, remaining butter and vinaigrette. Toss all the ingredients through the dressings and check the seasoning. Divide between hot bowls and serve with parmesan on the side.

In the bush

Barbecues

Barbecues are an essential part of summer life in Australia. Cooks everywhere are proud of their skills when it comes to grilling over a wood fire in the bush or over charcoal in the Weber on the verandah or in the backyard. Most of these cooks have their own theory on how to construct the best fire, what fuel to use and at what stage to commence placing the food on the grill so I will limit my advice to food matters.

For best cooking results, you need to build a really good fire that will hold its heat. The flames should have died down and the fire have formed a white ash. The flat grill must be very hot and clean so the food will not stick to it. If the grill is not hot enough, the food will not seal on the outside and will begin stewing in its own juices. The distance of the food from the heat source is also important, too close and the food could char and burn, and too far away and the food will barely cook. To prevent juices leaching out of the food while grilling I tend to season the food after it has finished cooking.

Timing is also very important as grilling is a fast cooking technique. I think grills should be simple dishes so the cooking of the main ingredient is very important. The success with dishes such as the Grilled sardines with herbs; the Grilled calamari with red serrano chilli and vinaigrette; and the Grilled Prawns with tarragon and garlic butter, is in removing the food almost as soon as it has been sealed on both sides. A simple dressing with lemon and butter or olive oil completes the dish. These easy dishes are extremely popular and often the best.

Barbecues conjure up relaxing times spent with friends. So even the more involved garnishes included here such as the zucchini, rosemary and anchovy with the lamb; potatoes with the beef; mushrooms and garlic with the duck; and the lime, ginger and pasta for the scallops, are kept simple. One of the secrets to grilling is preparation and organisation before you begin placing food on the grill. Then everything will come together at the last minute, and you can relax.

RIGHT: Grilled prawns with tarragon and garlic butter (recipe overleaf)

Grilled prawns
with tarragon and garlic butter

A perfect blend of ever-popular flavours. Buy the best prawns you can—everything here is simple and depends on the best produce. For the prawns to remain succulent and flavoursome only cook them until they are just beginning to turn opaque and remove from the heat immediately. The heated prawns will continue to cook a little and the warm sauce will complete the process.

Ingredients

Tarragon and garlic butter

5 tablespoons of water

1½ tablespoons fresh lemon juice, strained

2 teaspoons minced garlic

150 g butter, chilled and diced

2 teaspoons red serrano or similar hot chilli, seeded, finely chopped

1½ tablespoons fresh tarragon leaves

1 tablespoon chopped fresh flat-leaf parsley,

Sea salt and freshly ground black pepper

42 prawns, heads removed, shells on

Salt and freshly ground black pepper

5 tablespoons olive oil

1 lemon, cut into 6 wedges

Serves 6

To make the tarragon and garlic butter, place the water, ½ tablespoon of lemon juice, garlic and 30 g of butter in a small stainless steel saucepan over a medium heat. Bring to a boil and leave to combine for 20 seconds. Then turn the heat low and whisk in the butter in nut-size pieces, a little at a time. When all the butter is combined, add the chilli, tarragon and parsley and season with salt and pepper. Add the remaining lemon juice to taste and reserve the sauce in a warm place.

To cook the prawns, butterfly them, that is, split them not quite through lengthwise and open them out like a butterfly. Remove the intestine, wash and dry the prawns thoroughly and season with salt and pepper. Preheat the grill or barbecue to hot. Brush the hot plate with olive oil and place the prawns along the grill, flesh-side first, to quickly seal. Turn the prawns over and finish cooking. The prawns cook quickly so be careful to remove them when they are still slightly translucent. Reserve them on a warm serving platter. Alternatively, you can pour some of the butter over the prawns and grill them under a hot grill or salamander, again being careful not to overcook.

To serve, reheat the butter-sauce very gently if it is not still warm and spoon over the prawns. Place the platter in the centre of the table and serve with the lemon wedges.

SAUCE TIP
Add a very small pinch of fine dry breadcrumbs to the butter-sauce once it's finished and whisk to bind. This will help the sauce mask the prawns a little more while they are grilling.

Grilled calamari
with red serrano chilli vinaigrette

Sometimes the simplest things are the best and tastiest. Serve the grilled chilli calamari with some bitter greens.

Ingredients

Red serrano chilli vinaigrette

8 red serrano or similar hot chillies, seeded, finely chopped

3 teaspoons minced garlic

Sea salt and freshly ground black pepper

2 tablespoons lemon juice

1 cup extra-virgin olive oil

6 calamari, medium size

Olive oil

Fresh chives, snipped

1 lemon, cut into wedges

Serves 6

To make the chilli vinaigrette, place the chilli, garlic, seasoning and lemon juice in a bowl and gradually whisk in the olive oil until well blended. Infuse for a least an hour. Check the seasoning and acidity balance.

To clean the calamari, with your hands pull the head and the tentacles out and away from the tube. Remove the tentacles by cutting them off with a sharp knife in one piece just below the eyes. From the tube pull out the transparent backbone and the insides and discard. Peel off the side flaps and skin. Trim a little of the calamari from the pointed end. The idea is to end up with a cylinder and the tentacles. Wash the cylinder and tentacles well on the inside making sure no debris left, drain and dry well.

To cook the calamari, preheat the grill until very hot, brush the grill with a little oil and place the calamari bodies and tentacles on the hot grill. Cook for one minute and then turn the tubes over. Continue cooking for another minute and then, with the point of a very sharp knife, cut down the calamari lengthwise to open it up into a flat piece. Flip the calamari over, finish cooking quickly on the thin side and remove them and the tentacles to a warm platter.

To serve, spoon the chilli vinaigrette over the calamari making sure you serve the chilli flesh as well as the liquid. Place the calamari and juices onto warm serving plates and sprinkle with the chives and pepper. Serve with lemon wedges and plenty of crusty bread to mop up the juices.

Grilled white scallops with lime,
ginger and coriander

Lightly grilled scallops surrounding a bed of angel hair pasta and a fine julienne of ginger, cucumber and carrot are topped with coriander and chervil sprigs. The lime zest adds piquancy. Perfect for a quickly prepared meal after a day at the beach.

Ingredients

Sauce

½ cup white wine

2 golden shallots, peeled and finely chopped

1¼ cups extra-virgin olive oil

2½ tablespoons lemon juice

Sea salt and freshly ground black pepper

3 cm piece fresh ginger, peeled, finely julienned and
   blanched for 1 minute

½ Lebanese cucumber, finely julienned

1 carrot, julienned

150 g angel hair pasta (vermicelli), cooked and refreshed

2 tablespoons fresh coriander leaves, chopped

Olive oil

30 white scallops, cleaned and pat-dried

Olive oil

Zest of 1 lime

2 tablespoons fresh baby coriander sprigs

2 tablespoons fresh chervil sprigs

Serves 6

To make the sauce, combine the white wine and shallots in a stainless steel saucepan. Bring to a simmer over a low heat and reduce to 2½ tablespoons. Remove from the heat and whisk in the extra-virgin olive oil and lemon juice. Season to taste and reserve.

To make the pasta garnish, mix together the ginger, cucumber, carrot, angel hair pasta and chopped coriander leaves in a bowl and season lightly. Place in a steamer bowl and reserve. Heat the water for the steamer ready to reheat the garnish when needed.

To cook the scallops, preheat a flat top grill or two teflon pans with a little oil. When the grill or teflon pans are very hot grill the scallops over a high heat. Leave the scallops on the first side until they lightly caramelise, about 2 minutes, before turning them over and cooking very lightly on the second side. Remove from the grill and season with salt and pepper and reserve in a warm place. Spoon over some of the prepared sauce to mix with the scallop juices. Meanwhile steam the vegetable and pasta garnish for 1 minute.

To serve, compose a mound of the vegetable and pasta garnish in the centre of each warm plate. Place 5 scallops around the garnish and spoon over the juices and the sauce. Sprinkle the scallops with a little lime zest and decorate each vegetable and pasta garnish with baby coriander and chervil sprigs. Serve immediately.

SCALLOPS

When buying scallops make sure they have been carefully handled by the fishmonger. They should feel a little sticky and must be dry—not soaked in ice or water. Scallops are like a sponge and soak up moisture. The secret to successful cooking is their dryness which allows you to caramelise the first side on the hot grill.

LEFT: Grilled white scallops with lime, ginger and coriander

Grilled rib-eye steak
with rosemary potatoes, anchovy and tarragon butter

Serve this heady mixture of steak, anchovy and herbs with grilled field mushrooms or a large bowl of garden salad and a ripe Barossa shiraz.

Ingredients
Rosemary potatoes

8 potatoes (bintjes, kipflers, russet burbanks, desirees are good)

2 tablespoons chopped fresh rosemary leaves

Salt and freshly ground black pepper

½ cup olive oil

8 350–g x 3 cm thick rib-eye steaks on the bone, trimmed

6 tablespoons reduced Veal stock (page 132)

Anchovy and tarragon butter (page 129)

Landcress or watercress, picked

Serves 8

To prepare the potatoes, preheat the oven to 200°C. Slice the potatoes lengthwise into 1 cm slices and season with salt and pepper. Place the potatoes on an oiled flat baking tray, preferabley teflon, and sprinkle the rosemary over. Roast in the hot oven for 8–10 minutes on the first side or until they have begun to colour lightly. Remove the tray from the oven, turn the potatoes over with tongs, return to the oven and continue roasting on the second side until a light golden brown, about 5–6 minutes. Remove and keep warm or put aside to be reheated later while you cook the steaks.

To cook the steaks, brush olive oil over the steaks on both sides. Place on the hot grill and seal—that is, when a light beading of juice appears on the top side the underside is sealed. Turn the steaks over and continue cooking until they are done to your taste.

When the meat and potatoes are cooked, place the potatoes on warm plates or a large platter and season with salt and pepper. Place the meat on a cutting board and cut each steak into four slices, season and place over the potatoes. Top with slices of the anchovy and tarragon butter, pour over the hot veal stock and put a garnish of landcress on the side of the plate or platter. Serve immediately.

Grilled sirloin with caramelised onions
and field mushrooms

Everyone loves the smell of onions caramelising. In this recipe I have used a little sugar to enhance the onions' natural sweetness as they reduce down. Adding vinegar helps to balance this sweetness and the veal stock brings the dish together.

Ingredients

Caramelised onions

3 tablespoons olive oil

4 red onions, very finely sliced

2 tablespoons sugar

2 tablespoons white-wine vinegar + extra

¾ cup white wine

3 cups Veal stock (page 132)

3 fresh thyme sprigs

Sea salt and freshly ground black pepper

8 large field or flat mushrooms

4 tablespoons olive oil

2 teaspoons minced garlic

8 300–g sirloin steaks, cut 7–8 cm thick

2 tablespoons unsalted butter

2 tablespoons freshly chopped flat-leaf parsley

Serves 8

To prepare the caramelised onions, heat the 3 tablespoons of olive oil in a large frying pan over a medium heat. Add the onions and cook for 3 minutes, stirring frequently. Add the sugar, increase the heat to medium-high and cook the onions, stirring frequently until they caramelise, about 8–10 minutes. They should be a rich golden colour. Add the vinegar and increase the heat to high and reduce for 30 seconds. Add the wine and reduce for another minute. Then add the veal stock and thyme, reduce the heat to medium and simmer for 12–15 minutes. Season with salt and pepper and set aside.

To cook the mushrooms, preheat the grill or barbecue to a high heat. Brush both sides of the mushrooms with olive oil and place on the hot grill, top down. Spread a little garlic on each mushroom and leave to cook for 3–4 minutes before turning and cooking for a few minutes more or until they are tender. When they are cooked, remove the mushrooms to the very edge of the grill to keep warm.

To cook the steaks, grill them at the same time, sealing them on the first side until a light beading of juices appears on the top, about 5–6 minutes. Turn the steaks over and continue cooking until medium rare, about 2–3 minutes. Remove the steaks from the grill, season with salt and pepper and let them rest for 5 minutes on a tray in a warm place.

To serve, reheat the caramelised onions and swirl in the butter for a final blending. Season with salt and pepper and add a dash of vinegar, if needed, to give the onions a little lift. Place a mushroom on each plate and sprinkle with the parsley. Place a steak on or beside each mushroom, add any juices left from the resting beef to the onions, and spoon the onions and sauce over the steaks. Serve with Rosemary potatoes (page 84) if desired.

Grilled sardines with herbs,
garlic and lemon

A great barbecue dish—nothing could be simpler and yet the taste is heavenly. The rich taste of sardines cooked quickly over a flat grill is enhanced with fresh herbs and lemon. I have always preferred sardines when they have been cooked quickly and have retained their succulence.

Ingredients

20 fresh sardines

2 tablespoons minced garlic

Sea salt and freshly ground black pepper

2 tablespoons fresh flat-leaf parsley, coarsely chopped

2 tablespoons fresh thyme leaves

1 tablespoon chopped fresh rosemary leaves

4 tablespoons olive oil

2 tablespoons extra-virgin olive oil

1 lemon, cut in wedges

Serves 4

To prepare the sardines, cut off the head and tails and flip the sardine onto its back. Grab the backbone at the head end of the sardine, lift and pull upwards to release the whole bony spine in one piece. Scrape away any fine rib bones with a knife. After one or two sardines it will become very easy to fillet them. Place the filleted sardines skin side down on a flat tray side-by-side and smear each of them with a little garlic. Season with pepper and sprinkle over the herbs, then brush with a little oil and leave for a few minutes.

To cook the sardines, preheat a flat-top or grated grill plate to very hot and brush a little oil over evenly. Now here's the trick—working quickly, place the sardines herb-side down, on the grill, turning them over in the same order as previously. Then as soon as you have turned the last one, begin removing them from the grill, starting with the first fillet.

To serve, place the just-cooked juicy sardines onto a large warm platter, sprinkle with sea salt, drizzle with extra-virgin olive oil and serve with lemon wedges, fresh crusty bread or even grilled polenta (page 133).

VARIATIONS

Serve Samfaina (page 25) on the side or sprinkle over a little Preserved lemon (page 39). Serve with a salad and lots of crusty bread and you have a quick light lunch.

CHOPPING HERBS

Most herbs are delicate and require only gently chopping or slicing otherwise they will bruise and most of the flavour and juices will end up flavouring the chopping board instead of the dish. Gently chop parsley, thyme, rosemary and chervil. Slice basil, coriander and similar herbs with a sharp knife. Some herbs like chives are best snipped with sharp scissors.

RIGHT: Grilled sardines with herbs, garlic and lemon

Grilled lamb loin
with zucchini and garlic,
anchovy and rosemary vinaigrette

A simple lamb barbecue, the zucchini and lamb are greatly enhanced by the anchovy and rosemary dressing. Have everything ready in advance so it's ready to eat within minutes.

Ingredients

Anchovy and rosemary vinaigrette

2 tablespoons fresh rosemary leaves

15 anchovy fillets, rinsed

1¾ cups Lemon vinaigrette (page 129)

Lamb spice mix

1 tablespoon black peppercorns

1½ tablespoons white peppercorns

2 teaspoons cayenne pepper

2½ tablespoons mustard seeds

1½ tablespoons maldon sea salt flakes

1½ tablespoons fennel seeds

6 lamb loins, trimmed of all fat and sinew

Olive oil

Fresh rosemary sprigs

12 small zucchinis

2 teaspoons minced garlic

Sea salt and freshly ground black pepper

3 tablespoons chopped fresh flat-leaf parsley

Serves 6

To prepare the anchovy vinaigrette, put the rosemary, anchovy and lemon vinaigrette in a blender and purée until completely blended. Reserve.

To make the lamb spice mix, place all the ingredients in the blender or spice mill and blend well until the mixture is quite fine. Keep stored in a airtight jar in the refrigerator.

To cook the lamb, preheat the grill, season the lamb loins on both sides with the spice mix and brush both sides with olive oil. Place them on the hot grill and surround with rosemary sprigs. Turn the lamb over once it begins to show juice beads on the topside (that means the underside is sealed) and finish cooking the lamb to your taste. Remove the lamb from the grill and leave in a warm place to rest for 5 minutes.

Meanwhile, slice the zucchinis and heat 2 tablespoons of the olive oil in a frying pan. Place over the grill until the oil is nearly smoking. Add the minced garlic and the sliced zucchini. Sauté the zucchini, tossing regularly—it will cook quickly, about 2 minutes. Season with salt and pepper and toss with the parsley.

To serve, place a pile of zucchini in the centre of each plate. Slice the lamb in half lengthwise and place on the zucchini, spoon the rosemary and anchovy vinaigrette liberally over the lamb and on top of and around the plate and serve immediately.

Variation

Add some Tomato sauce (page 136) and Roasted garlic (page 91) beside the zucchini for another good blend of flavours.

Lamb cutlets
with spinach, pine nuts and sultanas

I usually prefer to use lamb loins or rib-eye from the rack, but cutlets are readily available and a succulent cut of meat if they are cooked quickly and served pink in the centre. Double cutlets are even better if you can persuade your butcher to cut them for you. Cutlets are easy to barbecue or grill and here they combine deliciously with the spinach, sultanas and pine nuts.

Ingredients

12 lamb cutlets, trimmed of excess fat

6 tablespoons olive oil

50 g unsalted butter

5 egg-shaped (roma) tomatoes, peeled, seeded, chopped

10 anchovy fillets, mashed with a fork

700 g spinach leaves, washed and drained

3 tablespoons sultanas, soaked in water, drained

2 tablespoons pine nuts, dry roasted

Sea salt and freshly ground black pepper

Serves 4

To cook the spinach, preheat the grill to hot and heat a heavy-bottomed frying pan with 3 tablespoons of olive oil and the butter. Add the tomatoes to the pan and cook the tomatoes until they have softened and collapsed. Add the anchovies, stir in and cook for another 30 seconds. Add the spinach leaves and sultanas and cook, stirring the leaves for about 2 minutes to wilt the spinach. Add the pine nuts and season with salt and pepper. Keep warm.

To cook the lamb, oil the preheated grill with the remaining olive oil and seal the lamb cutlets on the first side to brown well, about 2 minutes. Turn the cutlets and continue cooking for another minute or so. The cutlets should remain pink in the centre. Remove the lamb from the grill, season with salt and pepper, and rest the meat on a large plate for 2 minutes.

To serve the lamb, place the warm spinach in the centre of each plate. Place three lamb cutlets around the spinach and serve.

Grilled duck breast
with mushrooms and roasted garlic

The roasted garlic can be prepared ahead of time and reheated on the grill.

Ingredients
Roasted garlic
2 heads of garlic, cut in half crosswise, not peeled
2 tablespoons extra-virgin olive oil
Sea salt and freshly ground black pepper
4 sprigs fresh thyme

6 duck breasts, skin on, trimmed
2 tablespoons olive oil
300 g mushrooms, trimmed, stalks removed
1 tablespoon chopped fresh thyme leaves
4 tablespoons chopped flat-leaf parsley
5 tablespoons reduced veal stock (page 132), warmed, optional

To prepare the roasted garlic, preheat the oven to 190°C. Line a baking sheet with baking paper. Drizzle the cut side of each garlic half with the extra-virgin olive oil, season and top with a thyme sprig. Place the garlic on the sheet, cut-side down, and roast for 1 hour until the cloves are tender and pop out easily from the peel.

To prepare the duck, preheat the flat-top barbecue grill to very hot. Lightly oil the grill and place the duck breasts, skin side down, on the grill and cook until the skin is beautifully browned and crisp, about 5–10 minutes, depending on the thickness of the duck breasts. Turn the breasts and cook for another 3 minutes to keep the meat pink. Transfer to a plate and let them rest for a few minutes in a warm place.

Meanwhile, cook the mushrooms. Season and place them on the hot grill. Cook until cooked through then cut them into smaller pieces while still on the grill. Add the peeled garlic cloves, thyme and parsley and mix through the mushrooms to warm and infuse the mixture.

To serve, place a spoonful of the mushroom and garlic mixture on each plate and top with a duck breast, skin side up. Pour over any juices accumulated on the resting plate. Serve with a little warm reduced veal stock if desired.

GRILLING A DUCK BREAST
Use the same technique as grilling a steak. Leave the duck on the grill, skin side down, long enough to render its fat and become golden brown before turning to grill the other side. Thick Muscovy duck breasts are the best for grilling.

LEFT: Grilled duck breast with mushrooms and roasted garlic

RIGHT: Grilled quails with hummus, chickpea salad and paprika oil (overleaf)

Grilled quails with hummus,
chickpea salad and paprika oil

A great barbecue dish—you can have all the accompaniments ready and assemble it at the last minute while the quails are still grilling. The quail and their juices mingle deliciously with the hummus and salad.

Ingredients

Hummus

3 tablespoons tahini

3 tablespoons lemon juice + extra

2 teaspoons minced garlic

2 cups cooked Chick peas, skins removed (page 63)

½ cup reserved cooking liquid or water

Sea salt

½ teaspoon cumin

Pinch paprika

6 quails

Spice mixture

1 tablespoon cumin seeds

1 tablespoon coriander seeds

1 tablespoon sweet paprika

1 tablespoon freshly ground black peppercorns

½ tablespoon fennel seeds

3 tablespoons olive oil

¾ cup Lemon vinaigrette (page 129)

1 tablespoon Paprika oil (page 128)

1 cup Chick peas, cooked (page 63), outer skins removed

9 cherry tomatoes, halved

2 tablespoons pine nuts, dry roasted

2 tablespoons fresh coriander leaves

½ cup Salad of herbs (page 139) or fresh chervil sprigs

Serves 6 as a starter or 3 as a main

To make the hummus, place the tahini, lemon juice and garlic in the bowl of a food processor and blend for 1 minute. Add the chick peas and with the motor running, drizzle in the cooking liquid or water. Purée until well blended. Remove and push through a wire sieve with the aid of a wooden 'mushroom' or spatula. Correct the seasoning with salt, cumin, paprika and lemon juice. The hummous keeps well in an airtight container in the refrigerator. Return to room temperature before using.

To prepare the quails they must first be butterflied. Place the quail breast down on a cutting board with the legs facing you and cut through the cavity the length of the bird on either side of the backbone. Remove the backbone. The two halves are then opened and pressed flat to resemble a butterfly shape. With the skin side down, remove the rib cage by running your fingers between the flesh and the bones to release them. Cut through the wing and breast bones and remove the bones. Flatten out the quail further and cut the ends from the thigh and leg bones.

To make the spice mixture, place all the spice ingredients in a blender and grind to a powder. Sprinkle each quail on both sides with the spice mixture and place in an airtight container with the olive oil and leave to marinate for at least 1 hour in the refrigerator. Preheat the barbecue or grill.

Grill the quails, skin side down first, for 2–3 minutes until they begin to brown. Keep them moist by brushing with leftover marinade. Turn them over and complete the cooking for about 1 minute, checking the thighs which will take the longest to cook. Remove the quails from the grill, place on a tray and sprinkle with a little lemon vinaigrette and put aside to rest for 1–2 minutes in a warm place.

Continued overpage

Meanwhile, spread some hummus into the centre of each plate and make a well, sprinkle the hummus with a little paprika oil and lemon vinaigrette. Toss the chick peas, cherry tomatoes, pine nuts and coriander leaves in a bowl with some lemon vinaigrette and arrange around the hummus. Top with the rested quails and their juices. Toss the herb salad with some lemon vinaigrette and arrange some on each quail.

Quails grilled in vine leaves
with fig salad

A quick barbecue grill, especially if you have access to a grapevine. Be sure to pick the tender, fine young vine leaves.

Ingredients

24 fresh vine leaves

12 quails

Sea salt and freshly ground black pepper

1 cup olive oil

6 fresh ripe figs

⅖ cup extra-virgin olive oil

1 tablespoon balsamic vinegar

2 cups curly endive, white part only

1 cup lamb's lettuce (mâche) or watercress

3 tablespoons walnuts, roasted, chopped

Serves 6

To prepare the vine leaves, bring a large saucepan of water to the boil. You need to pick young tender vine leaves large enough to cover a quail breast. Place the vine leaves in the boiling water and cook for 30–60 seconds. Remove and lay out on a tray lined with a tea towel, to drain.

To prepare the quails, split them either side of the backbone the length of the quail and discard the bone. Open out the quail, like a butterfly, and flatten it by pressing hard on the breastbone. Cut off the wingtips. Sprinkle the quails with a little salt and pepper and place a vine leaf on either side of each quail breast. Place the finished quails on a tray and drizzle with the olive oil, cover with cling wrap and refrigerate for at least 3 hours.

To cook the quails, preheat the grill or barbecue to hot. Drain the quails of excess olive oil, and place on the grill plate, skin side down, and grill for about 3 minutes. Turn the quails over and cook on the second side for about 2 minutes or until golden, but still juicy.

Meanwhile, prepare the salad by cutting each fig into 6 segments and divide among the plates. Mix the extra-virgin olive oil and balsamic vinegar together and season with a little salt and pepper. Toss the endive and lamb's lettuce with just enough dressing to lightly coat the salads and place over the figs. Sprinkle over the walnuts.

To serve, remove the quails from the grill and place on a large platter or tray to rest for a minute. Place two quails on each plate and drizzle with a little more dressing and any quail juices remaining on the platter.

The sound of summer

Cicada dishes for special occasions

I couldn't write a cookbook without including some of my favourite recipes served at our restaurant. So although this chapter has been subtitled 'dishes for special occasions', all the recipes are very accessible. A thoughtful reading of the recipes and a little organised preparation will give you an insight into some of the skills and techniques employed in restaurant kitchens.

Recipes such as the Marinière of seafood with white beans and pistou and the Peppered beef with spinach and oyster mushrooms require a little last-minute juggling and combining just before serving so plan carefully. Some of these recipes, however, can all be prepared in advance—try the Escalivada terrine, Black-olive bread, and Calves brains with gribiche sauce.

The Banana galette uses techniques such as the Filo pastry and Crème patissière for which you will find everlasting uses. These are techniques that have been finely honed in the kitchens of Cicada. Good professional chefs are always searching for ways to refine and perfect basic elements of dishes that we know will work day-after-day and provide the platforms from which to launch the imagination. The Crème patissiere recipe has been arrived at after years of testing. I've always been happy with the taste but the perfect consistency took a while longer.

Much of the intrigue of cooking is finding the perfect balance of harmonising flavours in a dish. The Prawn ravioli and its accompanying sauce of ginger, soy and coriander comes close to this when all the elements of the dish are cooked correctly. When the pasta is only just-cooked through; the prawns are sweet and perfectly cooked; and the sauce has all its elements of heat, acid, spice and salt in balance, you are definitely close. When cooking ravioli you need to experiment with a few first to gauge the correct cooking time. I've suggested three minutes in this recipe, but set the timer and determine the perfect time in your kitchen, with your saucepan and heat source.

RIGHT: Passionfruit soufflé (recipe overleaf)

Passionfruit soufflé

When we purchased Le Trianon Restaurant, later renamed Cicada, in 1987. Le Trianon had a tradition and reputation for soufflés. I decided to continue the tradition and soufflés have been on the menu ever since. Passionfruit soufflé is one of our most popular—this recipe takes the mystery out of making them.

Ingredients

15 fresh passionfruit or 150 ml strained passionfruit juice

½ cup sugar syrup (page 140)

⅖ cup water

1½ tablespoons cornflour

1 tablespoon unsalted butter, softened

3 tablespoons caster sugar

10 eggwhites

Pinch cream of tartar

1½ tablespoons caster sugar

Serves 6

WHISKING EGGWHITES
Before you begin to whisk eggwhites make sure that the bowl and the whisk is spotlessly clean and dry. Bring the eggwhites to room temperature for about an hour.

To make the soufflé base, cut the passionfruit in half, scoop out all the pulp and place the pulp in a food processor bowl. Using the pulse button, purée to loosen the seeds from the pulp and juices. Don't purée too hard or the seeds will be blended and broken up. Remove the purée to a sieve placed over a bowl and strain all the juices, pushing down hard on the pulp to extract as much juice as possible. You will need 150 ml of strained passionfruit juice.

Put the passionfruit juice, sugar syrup and water in a saucepan and mix together—this is the base mixture. Place the cornflour in a smaller bowl and dissolve it in ¼ cup of the base mixture. Bring the base mixture to the boil over high-heat. Whisk in the dissolved cornflour slurry and blend well. Continue whisking and bring the base mixture back to a boil to thicken and continue cooking for 2 minutes, whisking constantly. The mixture should be boiling rapidly. Remove from the heat and pour it into a container and cover with cling-film pressed onto the surface of the mixture to prevent a skin from forming (the soufflé can be prepared ahead of time up to this point). Preheat the oven to 200°C.

Take six soufflé moulds, grease the sides with the softened butter and making sure all sides are completely covered. Sprinkle into each mould 3 tablespoons of caster sugar and twist the moulds to coat the sides with a fine even layer of sugar. Invert the mould and tip the sugar into another mould and repeat until all the moulds are coated. Tip out the excess sugar and discard. It's important that the moulds are evenly coated with butter and sugar right to the top as this helps the soufflé rise up the sides of the mould without sticking.

Place the soufflé-base mixture in a bowl and whisk to blend. Put the eggwhites and cream of tartar in a clean, dry, large bowl and whisk to a soft snow adding the 1½ tablespoons of caster sugar towards the end. Aim for a stage between soft peaks and stiffened whites as these whites will fold in better. Spoon a quarter of the egg-whites into the base mixture and fold in with a rubber spatula. Add the remaining whites and fold in gently. Fill the soufflé dishes to the top and level the surface with a
Continued overleaf

metal spatula. Run your thumb around the inside edge of each mould so the soufflé will rise without catching.

Bake without opening the oven for 12–13 minutes. Check the soufflés; they may need another 1–2 minutes. As soon as they are ready serve with whipped cream. Passionfruit sorbet served separately is an excellent alternative (page 116).

Salmon paillard on shaved fennel,
mushroom and radish salad

A paillard is like a minute steak, a fish fillet in this case, sliced thinly and cooked very quickly. The beauty of cooking the salmon this way is that it stays very moist and retains a beautiful sheen. Finely shaved fennel retains all of its freshness, flavour and crunch—it's a great mixer. Choose tightly closed white mushrooms.

Ingredients

600 g salmon fillet

2 tablespoons Clarified butter (page 128)

¼ teaspoon white truffle oil

5 tablespoons Lemon vinaigrette

1 fennel bulb, trimmed

8 small, white button mushrooms, wiped clean

4 red radishes, washed, dried

Sea salt and freshly ground black pepper

2 tablespoons chopped fresh flat-leaf parsley

Serves 4

To the prepare the salmon, ask for the salmon in one piece, about 20 cm long. Cut the salmon in half across the fillet and then using a thin sharp filleting knife, cut through the fillet horizontally to divide it into two thin paillards. Repeat with the other piece of fillet to make 4 paillards. Paint 2 oven-proof, large flat plates lightly with clarified butter and place 2 paillards on each plate, side-by-side, with the nicest presentation side face up. Reserve.

To prepare the salad, mix the truffle oil with the lemon vinaigrette. Slice the fennel bulb in half vertically. Shave into very thin, fine shavings on a mandoline slicer and set aside. Slice the mushrooms very finely on the mandoline and add to the fennel. Then slice the radish very finely on the mandoline into rounds and add to the fennel and mushrooms. Season with salt and pepper and add the chopped parsley. Toss together with lemon vinaigrette and divide among 4 serving plates.

To cook the salmon, preheat the oven to 130°C. Place the 2 plates of salmon on the bottom of the oven—under the lowest shelf—and leave to cook for 2–3 minutes. The idea is that the heat of the plate will cook the salmon from the bottom up at a low even heat. The salmon is ready when it still has a fresh rare sheen on the top.

To serve, remove the salmon from the oven and carefully place a paillard on top of a mound of salad on the serving plates. Sprinkle the salmon with sea salt and serve with extra vinaigrette if desired.

Prawn ravioli with ginger and coriander

A clean-tasting dish, the sauce complements the prawn ravioli perfectly.

Ingredients

27 king prawns, shelled, de-veined, washed

18 coriander leaves

Sea salt and freshly ground black pepper

Ravioli pasta (page 134), rolled into sheets or Shanghai
   wonton wrappers

Ginger, soy and coriander sauce

5 cm-piece ginger, peeled, finely grated

2 tablespoons white wine

½ cup Court bouillon (page 29)

150 g unsalted butter, chilled, cut to large dice

1 tablespoon light soy sauce

2 teaspoons sherry vinegar

1 teaspoon chilli paste (or harissa)

20 fresh coriander leaves

1 tablespoon fine julienned ginger, blanched, refreshed

1½ tablespoons finely sliced green shallots

1 red serrano or similar hot chilli, seeded, finely chopped

Serves 6

To prepare the ravioli filling, slice each prawn lengthwise into halves. You need 3 prawn halves to make a bundle and you need 18 bundles to form 3 ravioli for each serve. Lay the 18 bundles on a cutting board then cut the prawns across into halves widthwise. Form a tight round bundle with each. Season these with salt and pepper and top each with a coriander leaf.

To prepare the prawn ravioli, lay the rolled pasta out on a floured bench and place each bundle of prawns evenly spaced down a strip of pasta every 12 cm. Brush the pasta with a little water around each bundle, and fold the pasta sheet over the top. Make a ravioli with the sides of your cupped hands—pressing down to seal the pasta. Press the edges well to seal and using a 9 cm round cutter, stamp out each ravioli and press out any air pockets. Repeat with the remaining pasta and prawn bundles. Keep the prepared ravioli between dry tea towels on a flat tray and refrigerate.

To prepare the sauce, place the finely grated ginger in a stainless steel saucepan and cover with the wine. Place over a medium heat and reduce to 2 tablespoons. Add the court bouillon and reduce by
Continued overleaf

LEFT: Prawn ravioli with ginger and coriander

RIGHT: Black potato gnocchi with calamari, peppers and chives (recipe overleaf)

two-thirds. Turn the heat to low, and whisk in the chilled butter, piece-by-piece, waiting until the first piece has been incorporated before adding the next piece. When all the butter is emulsified, balance the final taste of the sauce by adding soy sauce, sherry vinegar and chilli paste and taste for seasoning. All the flavouring ingredients of the sauce should be evident in the final sauce; the heat and spiciness of the ginger and chilli, the saltiness of the soy, and acidity of the vinegar play off each other. Strain the sauce through a fine sieve and keep warm.

To cook the ravioli, heat a large saucepan, or preferably two, with boiling, salted water over a high heat. Give the water a stir in one direction to create a whirlpool effect (this stops the ravioli diving straight to the bottom and clinging to the saucepan's base—not the desired result). Drop the ravioli in 6 to 9 at a time depending on the size of the saucepan. Give a stir occasionally, and cook for 3 minutes. Remove the ravioli to a tray lined with a tea towel to drain quickly.

To serve, arrange three ravioli on each warm serving bowl. Pour the sauce over the ravioli and top each with a little ginger, green shallots, chilli and coriander leaves. This dish is good served with hot, buttered cabbage or bok choy.

TOASTED OLIVE BREAD
When lightly toasted, black-olive bread is a perfect accompaniment for Escalivada terrine with tapenade (page 105) or the Grilled salad of roasted capsicums, anchovies and basil (page 56).

Black-olive bread

Mixing the olives into the dough at the beginning gives the bread a nice olive colour once it has been baked.

Ingredients

4¾ cups unbleached flour + extra

3½ teaspoons dried yeast

1 teaspoon sea salt

2 cups pitted black olives

¾ cup warm water

¼ cup olive oil

Makes 2 medium-sized loaves

To prepare the bread, add the flour, yeast, salt and olives to the bowl of an electric mixer with a hook attachment and mix on a low speed for 20 seconds. Add the water and olive oil to the bowl and continue mixing on a medium speed, kneading for 12 minutes.

Remove the dough from the bowl and place on a lightly floured bench and knead by hand for 3 minutes. Place the dough, formed into a ball, in a large, lightly floured bowl and cover with a damp tea towel. Keep in a warm place to double in size, for about 1½–2 hours.

Knock back the dough with your hands by punching down and reforming. Divide the dough into 2 loaf pans or terrine moulds, preferably Teflon, or form into 2 free-form loaves on a greased flat baking tray.

To bake the bread, place it in a preheated oven at 190°C for 15 minutes. Remove the bread from the oven, unmould, and place on a wire rack, quickly spray or sprinkle with a little water and return to the oven to finish baking for another 10 minutes. Remove from the oven and cool on a rack. If you wish to freeze one loaf, seal it well in a freezerbag, and freeze the bread while it is still slightly warm.

Black potato gnocchi with calamari

A great dish—visual, textural and very tasty. The soft potato gnocchi is blackened with squid ink and the calamari is cooked very quickly by a method I call 'cold poached' which makes it very tender.

Ingredients

Black potato gnocchi

500 g bintje or desiree potatoes

100 g flour + extra

1 tablespoon squid ink (available from fish mongers and fine delicatessens)

Squid ink sauce

1 tablespoon olive oil

2 garlic cloves, peeled, smashed

2 golden shallots, peeled, minced

2 sprigs fresh thyme

Reserved calamari trimmings as below

6 tablespoons white wine

4/5 cup Fish stock (page 131)

2/5 cup cream

2 tablespoons squid ink

Sea salt and freshly ground black pepper

1/2 cup white wine

1/2 cup Fish stock (page 131)

600 g calamari, cleaned, (page 81), sliced in very thin strips

1 Roasted red capsicum, diced (page 137)

3 tablespoons chopped fresh chives

Serves 10

TIME SAVER
All the preparation for this dish can be done in advance and brought together at the last moment. The cooked gnocchi, well drained, can be stored in the refrigerator or freezer.

To make the gnocchi, preheat the oven to 175°C. Bake the potatoes for 1 hour or until well cooked. Split the potatoes, scoop out the flesh and press through a potato ricer or sieve them well. Place the potato mash in a large bowl and mix in the flour and the squid ink, working quickly so as not to overwork the dough which would make the gnocchi heavy and sticky. The dough should feel smooth and barely sticky on the outside. Shape the dough into a ball and roll lightly in flour. Cut off a quarter of the dough and roll it out by hand on a lightly floured bench into a snake about 2 cm thick. Cut into 1–2 cm pieces and roll the pieces over a gnocchi paddle or the back of a fork to form a groove pattern. Place the gnocchi on a floured tray, cover and refrigerate.

To prepare the squid ink sauce, heat the olive oil over a low heat and add the garlic, shallots and thyme and sweat gently for 1–2 minutes. Add any calamari trimmings left over and cook for 2 minutes. Pour in the white wine, bring to a boil and reduce by half. Pour over the fish stock, boil and reduce by half. Add the cream and simmer for 3–4 minutes. Then add the squid ink and season. Strain the sauce through a sieve and reserve.

To cook the gnocchi, place small batches of gnocchi in a large saucepan of boiling water over a medium heat and as the gnocchi rises to the surface remove them with a sieve or slotted spoon. Place the cooked gnocchi in a warm bowl while you cook the rest.

Cook the calamari garnish while the gnocchi is cooking. Heat the white wine and fish stock with a pinch of salt in a saucepan and bring to a rolling boil over a high heat. Add the calamari strips and remove from the heat immediately and leave to cold poach for 1 minute, then strain the liquid off. Place the calamari in a warm bowl, add the capsicum dice and chives, season and keep warm. In a small frying pan reheat the squid ink sauce to a simmer and add the gnocchi to warm through.

To serve, spoon the gnocchi into warm bowls, add the calamari garnish and pour over enough sauce to coat the gnocchi well. Serve immediately.

Marinière of snapper,
calamari and scallops, tuscan beans and pistou

A taste of the sea in a bowl. Cooking the seafood this way keeps it moist and the broth and vegetables combined with the pistou have the most amazing aroma.

Ingredients

Sauce

3 cups Fish stock (page 131)

3 tablespoons extra-virgin olive oil

100 g butter, cold

2½ tablespoons fresh lemon juice, strained

Sea salt and freshly ground black pepper

10 50–g snapper fillets, skin on, boned

200 g White cannellini beans, cooked (page 63)

1 red capsicum, finely diced, blanched, refreshed

1 zucchini, green part only, finely diced

2 tomatoes, peeled, seeded, diced

1 carrot, peeled, finely diced, blanched, refreshed

20 scallops, cleaned and dried (page 26)

30 small octopus tentacles, cleaned (page 60)

30 calamari rings, cleaned (page 81)

3 tablespoons chopped fresh flat-leaf parsley

2½ tablespoons Pistou (page 29)

Fresh chervil sprigs

Serves 10

To make the sauce, place 1½ cups of the stock in a stainless steel saucepan over a medium heat and bring to a boil. Whisk in the extra-virgin olive oil then whisk in the butter. Add the lemon juice to taste, season and set aside.

To cook the seafood, place the remaining fish stock in another stainless steel saucepan with some salt, bring to the boil and maintain at a boil. Place the sauce in the first saucepan over a low heat and add the snapper, white beans and vegetable dice and heat until the fish is poached, about 3 minutes. Meanwhile add the scallops, octopus and calamari to the second saucepan and immediately remove from the heat and set aside to cold poach the contents, about 2 minutes.

To serve, drain the squid, octopus and calamari from the stock and add them to warmed serving bowls (reserve the stock for another dish). Divide the beans and vegetables between the bowls and top with a piece of snapper. Give the snapper sauce another quick boil, add the chopped parsley, and taste for seasoning. Pour the sauce over the seafood and vegetables and spoon in the pistou to finish. Top with chervil sprigs.

COOKING SEAFOOD STEWS

When cooking seafood dishes like the one above and other stews such as brodetto and bouillabaise, think carefully about how much time each piece of fish or shellfish takes to cook. Separate them into groups of cooking times and even use two saucepans if necessary. As the broth heats keep adding the seafood according to cooking time. A final combining of the ingredients and an adjustment to the seasoning will ensure the seafood has retained its succulence and flavour.

RIGHT: Marinière of snapper, calamari and scallops, tuscan beans and pistou

Roasted squab
with savoy cabbage and broad beans

Squab pigeons have lean dark flesh and a rich, slightly gamey flavour which make them a favourite of mine. Search for good quality squabs.

Ingredients

4 400–g squab pigeons

½ savoy cabbage

Sea salt and freshly ground black pepper

4 tablespoons Clarified butter (page 128)

2 tablespoons red-wine vinegar

⅖ cup reduced Veal stock (page 132)

3 tablespoons unsalted butter, chilled

1 cup broad beans, podded, blanched, shelled

Serves 4

SQUAB

Squab should be cooked no more than medium-rare to retain its juices and tenderness. Rest squab after cooking in a warm place to relax the flesh and redistribute the juices through the flesh. The flavour of squab seems to be infinately versatile and marries well with a wide range of vegetables and fruit. The bones make rich, full-flavoured stocks and soups.

To clean the squabs, cut away the outside wingtips with a sharp knife. Chop through the neck bones to remove the head. Trim any fat away from the flesh near the breastbone. Place the squabs on a tray layered with absorbent paper and leave, uncovered, in the refrigerator overnight. This helps dry out the bird and is a type of rendering process.

To prepare and blanch the cabbage, first remove all the outside tough, bruised leaves. Then remove the core and thick ribs by placing the cabbage on a cutting board with the stem uppermost and using a sharp, thin knife cut down and around the core to release the leaves from the centre core. Turn the cabbage over and peel off the leaves one-by-one. Lay them out flat on the cutting board and remove the thick, tough ribs. Finally cut the cabbage into a fine julienne. Bring a large saucepan of salted water to the boil and blanch the cabbage for 2–3 minutes. Refresh and drain the cabbage well and set aside.

To roast the squabs, preheat the oven to 260°C and season the birds all over. In a frying pan large enough to contain the four squabs, heat the clarified butter until very hot and add the squabs. Seal them on all sides then place them on their backbones, breast-side up, and roast in the preheated oven for 6–8 minutes. The squabs are best served pink. Remove them from the oven and leave to rest for 10 minutes, breast-side down, on a rack over a tray, in a warm place.

To make the sauce, pour the fat from the frying pan. Over a high heat, deglaze the pan with the vinegar, stir, scraping the pan and reduce the vinegar to 2 teaspoons. Add the veal stock, boil and reduce to a syrup over a high heat. Set aside.

When the squabs have rested for 10 minutes, remove the legs by cutting with a large sharp knife down between the side of the breast and the thigh bone. Set aside on a tray. Remove the breast by cutting along either side of the breastbone the length of the squab and cutting down through the wing bone. Place on the tray next to the legs. The squabs can be reheated in the hot oven for 1 minute just before serving. Meanwhile, reheat the cabbage in boiling salted water or steam it, then pour into a strainer and drain very well. Place in a small bowl and season with salt and pepper. Cabbage loves black pepper, so add extra to taste along with 2 tablespoons of butter and mix well to melt the butter and coat all of the cabbage. Reheat the broad beans, *Continued overleaf* separately, in the same hot water, or steamer for 1 minute. Season and toss with 1 tablespoon of butter.

Place the cabbage on the plate and spoon a pile of broad beans next to the cabbage. Place the squab legs next to the cabbage and top the cabbage and legs with the breast, spoon over a little reheated sauce and serve immediately. French green lentils from Puy would also enhance this dish.

Escalivada terrine with tapenade

Escalivada is a Spanish summer vegetable salad that is sometimes roasted and sometimes grilled. To make an elegant presentation I've pressed the roasted vegetables into a terrine so they retain their essential flavour.

Ingredients

Terrine

6 eggplants, sliced vertically into 13 mm slices

16 egg-shaped (roma) tomatoes, peeled, halved, seeded

3 fresh thyme sprigs, chopped

Sea salt and freshly ground black pepper

7 Roasted red capsicums (page 137), skinned

4 tablespoons Tapenade (page 32)

2 tablespoons capers

4 tablespoons small black olives

1 cup extra-virgin olive oil

2 tablespoons balsamic vinegar

1 loaf Black-olive bread (page 100), optional

Serves 12

To make the terrine, preheat the oven to 175°C. Arrange the eggplant slices on a flat baking tray lined with baking paper and roast in the oven for 12–15 minutes on each side. Remove from the oven and cool.

Lower the oven to 125°C. Place a wire rack on a flat tray and arrange the tomato halves, cut side down, on the rack. Sprinkle with thyme, season with salt and pepper and roast in the oven for 2½ hours. Remove when the tomatoes are quite dried and set aside to cool.

Line a small terrine mould with cling-wrap, allowing about 5 cm to extend over the sides. Place slices of eggplant very slightly overlapping in the terrine to cover the bottom. Add a layer of tomatoes and then another layer of eggplant. Cut the red capsicum to fit the terrine and place a layer on top of the eggplant. Add another layer of eggplant and then another layer of tomatoes. Cut another layer of eggplant, then capsicum, and repeat to the top of the mould, alternating eggplant layers between every tomato and capsicum layer. Press down well between layers with a spatula to ensure the layers fit into the terrine tightly. Finish with a layer of red capsicums. Fold the cling wrap from the sides over the filled terrine. To press the terrine, place a heavy weight on top. A piece of board cut to fit the terrine or a brick will do. Refrigerate overnight.

To serve the terrine, unmould the terrine by inverting it onto a cutting board and pulling down on the overhanging sides of the cling-wrap to release it. With a sharp knife, cut the terrine into 1.5 cm thick slices and place on serving plates. Arrange some tapenade, capers and olives beside the terrine and drizzle olive oil and balsamic vinegar over and around the terrine. Season and serve with olive bread.

Deep-fried calves' brains
with gribiche sauce

Crumbed brains and gribiche sauce is a classic combination. The gribiche sauce has great versatility—its brightness and zing will give a lift to ocean trout confit, grilled fish such as rouget (red mullet) and sardines and vegetable salads.

Ingredients

3 calves' brains, if unavailable use lambs' brains

Gribiche sauce

1 hard-boiled egg, separated, yolk chopped, white diced finely

1 tablespoon finely diced golden shallots

1 tablespoon chopped capers

1 tablespoon chopped cornichons (small gherkins)

1 teaspoon Dijon mustard

1½ tablespoons red-wine vinegar

½ cup extra-virgin olive oil

1 teaspoon finely diced fresh tarragon

1½ tablespoons chopped fresh flat-leaf parsley

1½ tablespoons snipped fresh chives

1 tablespoon chopped fresh chervil

Court bouillon (page 29)

Sea salt and freshly ground black pepper

1 tablespoon plain flour + extra

1 egg, beaten with 1 tablespoon water (eggwash)

1 cup fine fresh breadcrumbs

Canola or vegetable oil for deep-frying

24 fresh sage leaves, stems attached

1 lemon, cut into wedges

Serves 6

To clean the brains, soak them in cold, lightly salted water for 2 hours, changing the water 3 or 4 times. This will soften the membranes that cover them. Drain the brains and carefully remove the membrane with your fingers or the point of a knife, then soak them again to dissolve any blood. Drain and reserve in the refrigerator.

To prepare the gribiche sauce, place all the ingredients in a mixing bowl and carefully stir together. If you want to keep it for another day, leave out the sherry vinegar and add it just before serving. Return the sauce to room temperature to serve.

To prepare the brains, cook the court bouillon, strain it, add the cleaned brains and poach gently over a low-heat for 15 minutes or until firm to touch. Remove and drain well. Cut into manageable pieces and store, covered in the refrigerator until needed. Season the brains and toss in the flour, shaking to remove any excess, then toss them in the eggwash and finally toss them through the breadcrumbs until evenly coated.

To cook the brains, pour the oil into a deep saucepan, one-third full. Heat the oil to 185°C or test the oil with a breadcube—when the oil bubbles and the breadcube colours and crisps within a minute it is ready. Add the crumbed brains, a few at a time, and fry for 4–5 minutes or until golden brown. Remove and drain on absorbent paper and keep warm. When all the brains are cooked, add the sage leaves lightly dusted in extra flour to the oil and fry quickly until crisp.

To serve, spoon the gribiche sauce evenly onto the centre of the plates, top with a pile of calves' brains, add the sage leaves and serve with lemon wedges.

LEFT: Deep-fried calves' brains with gribiche sauce

Peppered beef fillet
with spinach and oyster mushrooms

This dish requires a little juggling at the finish line, but most of its components can be prepared ahead of time. It's a dish of finely balanced flavours which is well worth the effort.

Ingredients

Spice blend

3 tablespoons black peppercorns

3 tablespoons coriander seeds

1 tablespoon sea salt

6 200–g beef fillet, centre-cut if possible, trimmed

2 tablespoons olive oil

4 tablespoons Clarified butter (page 128)

1 cup oyster mushrooms, trimmed

1 teaspoon minced garlic

1 cup enoki mushrooms, trimmed

½ cup black wood-ear fungi, trimmed, rinsed, optional

2 cups spinach leaves, washed, blanched, refreshed, drained

Sea salt and freshly ground black pepper

12 thin baby leeks, trimmed, blanched, refreshed

½ cup reduced Veal stock (page 132), warm

Serves 6

To prepare the spice blend, place the ingredients in a blender and grind together. Aim for a not-too-finely processed mixture.

To cook the beef, preheat the oven to 220°C. Sprinkle the top and underside of each steak with the spice-crust blend. Heat the olive oil in a frying pan over a high heat. Add the beef fillets and sear on one side for 2 minutes, turn over and sear the second side for 1 minute. Remove from the stove and immediately place in the preheated oven to finish cooking, about 4–5 minutes for medium-rare. Remove from the oven and rest in a warm place for 5 minutes.

Meanwhile, prepare the vegetables by heating the clarified butter in a large saucepan over a high heat. Add the oyster mushrooms and minced garlic and cook for 1 minute. Then add the enoki mushrooms and wood-ear fungi and continue cooking until ready, about 1 minute. Add the blanched spinach and mix through the mushrooms to reheat and season with salt and pepper. At the same time, reheat the leeks in a steamer or on a buttered tray in the oven. Reheat the veal stock in a saucepan.

To serve the beef and vegetables, arrange the spinach and mushrooms in the centre of each warm plate. Top with the hot leeks and place a beef fillet on top of the leeks. Spoon over some veal sauce and serve.

Caramelised banana galette

A Cicada classic. The final fanning and glazing of the banana has to be done at the last minute but it is a technique quickly mastered.

Ingredients

6 filo pastry sheets

4 tablespoons unsalted butter, melted

2 tablespoons white almond meal

2 tablespoons caster sugar

Crème patissière (pastry cream)

2 cups milk

1 cup caster sugar + extra

1 teaspoon vanilla extract

5 egg yolks

1 egg

20 g flour

30 g cornflour

50 g unsalted butter, cut into pieces

4 ripe bananas

4 passionfruit

Serves 4

To make the filo galettes, line a flat baking tray with baking paper. Lay out a sheet of filo pastry and brush with melted butter. Sprinkle evenly and lightly with the almonds and sugar, lay another sheet of filo on top and press down firmly to compact the sheets. Repeat with the remaining sheets of filo leaving the top sheet dry. Place another baking sheet on top of the filo tray and refrigerate for 30 minutes. Remove the filo stack to a bench top or cutting board and cut out four, 100 cm diameter circles to form the galettes. Place on a flat baking tray, top with another tray and bake in a preheated oven at 175°C for 10 minutes or until the galette is golden brown. Remove from the oven and cool them on a rack. The galettes can be made ahead of time and kept in an airtight container.

To make the crème patissière, bring the milk, half the sugar and vanilla to the boil in a stainless steel saucepan over a high heat and reserve. In a stainless steel bowl, whisk the egg yolks and egg until they whiten and add the remaining sugar. Gradually add the flour and cornflour blending until smooth. Tip half the boiled milk onto the yolk mixture and whisk to blend. Working quickly, pour this mixture onto the milk in the saucepan. Return the saucepan to the high heat and whisk vigorously until the custard boils. Whisk for 30 seconds after it boils and remove from the heat. Scrape the custard into a mixing bowl and leave to cool for 3 minutes. Whisk the butter gradually into the warm custard until it is incorporated. Cover the pastry cream with cling wrap pressed into the surface. When cool, refrigerate.

To serve, spread a thin layer of pastry cream over the galette bases. Cut the peeled bananas diagonally into thin slices leaving the bananas close to their original shape on the cutting board. Pick up the first slice and lay it flat on the pastry cream, slightly overhanging the edge of the galette. Overlap the remaining slices of banana around the circular galette tucking the last one under the first slice. The banana slices should look evenly spaced and fanned. Sprinkle the bananas with an even layer of caster sugar and caramelise with a blowtorch or under a preheated very hot grill. Cut the passionfruit and spoon the pulp over the galettes. Place a scoop of ice-cream or sorbet in the centre of each galette.

The sweet life

Desserts and fruit

In early summer I immediately begin dreaming of the fruit that will be available throughout the season for desserts. I like to make summer desserts that are refreshing and light and I find that fruit provides the perfect foil for ice-creams, pastries and light sauces.

Tropical fruits, such as our world-famous, luscious mangoes, begin arriving in early summer and reach near perfection when ripe. Enhanced simply by a drizzle of lime or passionfruit and a little coconut ice-cream, they are even better. I think it's important that the fruit's essential flavour is not masked by trying to create an overly elaborate dessert. Treat the fruit as the star and add a complementary flavour in a supporting role. This can be achieved to great effect when you serve the fruit hot or warm. Sprinkle a perfectly ripe peach, nectarine or plum with a little sugar and grill it until it begins to glaze and caramelise. This will enhance the fruit's natural acidity and heighten its true flavour. Eaten with ice-cream, the contrast of hot and cold is divine. A warm compôte of cherries or berries with a sauce based on their own juices is another excellent taste.

Familiarise yourself with the many different varieties of peaches, nectarines, plums, raspberries, strawberries and other fruits. Many of the most aromatic and best-tasting summer fruits are very delicate. Good fruiterers often have a passion for these delicious varieties but are reluctant to handle them because of their fragility. By asking for specific varieties they may happily purchase tray quantities for you. Why not share a tray with a friend? The difference in perfume and taste can be astounding when comparing say, a raspberry grown in a cooler climate with naturally high acidity, with a lesser variety from a warm growing area.

Summer berries complement pastry perfectly so try the Raspberry and mascapone tarts and the Strawberry shortcakes. At the restaurant we always toss strawberries in a little orange or lemon juice and icing sugar to macerate them quickly. This is the best way to accentuate their flavour. Try them with the Moist orange-syrup cake. Fresh berries make wonderful sorbets, ice-creams and sauces for which you will find endless uses.

RIGHT: Almond and pistachio tart with grilled peaches (recipe overleaf)

Almond and pistachio tart
with grilled peaches

The perfect summer evening dessert. A light, easy-to-make tart served with caramelised grilled peaches.

Ingredients

500 g Sweet pastry (page 113)

Flour for dusting

225 g unsalted butter, softened

1 cup caster sugar

1 cup ground white almond

½ cup ground pistachios

5 small eggs

½ cup flour

Pinch ground cinnamon

4–5 freestone peaches (or nectarines or plums), halved, seeded, skin on

3 tablespoons caster sugar

Icing sugar for dusting

1 cup thick double cream

Serves 8–10

To prepare the tart case, remove the pastry from the refrigerator and allow it to soften a little, about 8 minutes. Place the pastry on a lightly floured surface and shape into a round with your fingers. Lightly flour the rolling pin and roll out the pastry lifting and turning it frequently and lightly and flouring the work surface as needed to prevent sticking. Roll out until it is large enough to line the tart mould (24 cm diameter). Lift the pastry on top of the rolling pin to the tart case and gently press the pastry into the case. Trim off the excess pastry. Return to the refrigerator to rest overnight or for 2 hours.

To cook the tart, preheat the oven to 180°C. Put the softened butter in the bowl of an electric mixer and beat until it is light and creamy. Add the caster sugar and beat the mixture until it whitens and is fluffy. Add the almonds and pistachios and blend well. Add the eggs one at a time. Add the flour and cinnamon and blend them in. Pour this mixture into the prepared tart ring and cook in the oven for 30 minutes. Check the tart—it should have risen and should be quite firm in the centre. Remove from the oven and place on a cake rack to cool.

To cook the peaches, place the peach halves, cut side up, on a tray and dab with absorbent paper to soak up excess juice. Sprinkle well with the caster sugar and place under a hot grill. Grill until the sugar begins to caramelise the peaches, and they begin to colour. Remove and finish cooking in the oven for 4–5 minutes if the peaches are still a little firm. Slice the tart into wedges, dust the top with icing sugar and serve with the peaches and thick double cream.

Raspberry and mascarpone tarts
with raspberry sorbet

Raspberries on raspberries with raspberries, enhanced with mascarpone. Try to buy raspberries grown in cool-climate regions—they have an acidity-enhanced depth of flavour. I like working with small tartlettes as rolling the pastry and lining the tart moulds is so easy.

Ingredients

Sweet pastry

200 g unsalted butter

1⅓ cups icing sugar, sifted

2 eggs

3¾ cups flour

Raspberry purée

3½ cups fresh raspberries, hulled

Raspberry sorbet

2½ cups raspberry purée, strained and chilled

1¼ cup Sugar syrup (page 140), chilled

Raspberry sauce

3 tablespoons raspberry purée, strained

2 tablespoons sugar syrup

½ cup mascarpone

¼ cup sour cream

½ teaspoon lemon zest

2 tablespoons icing sugar, sifted

1½ cups raspberries

Serves 8

To prepare the sweet pastry, soften the butter by beating it on a bench with a rolling pin. Place it in the bowl of an electric mixer and continue to soften it with the paddle attachment. Add the icing sugar and blend well. Add the eggs one at a time and blend again. Turn the speed to low and add the flour to just mix. Remove the dough from the bowl and place on a floured bench. Work the pastry with the heel of your palm across the bench once for a final blending. Gather into a ball, flatten, wrap in cling-film and refrigerate for 1–2 hours.

To prepare the raspberry purée, place the raspberies in a food processor and purée until blended. Pour into a fine sieve placed over a bowl and push the purée through with a wooden mushroom to extract all the juices. Discard the seeds. Chill in the refrigerator.

To cook the tart bases, remove the pastry and allow to soften a little. Roll out small pieces just large enough to line your small tart moulds (80 cm diameter) on a floured bench. Press the pastry into the moulds, trim, and return to the refrigerator to rest for 30 minutes before baking. Preheat the oven to 180°C, remove the tarts, prick the bottom of the pastry with a fork and cook until golden brown, about 8–10 minutes. Remove and cool. Keep them in an airtight container for up to 2 days.

To make the raspberry sorbet, mix 1½ cups of chilled raspberry purée with the chilled syrup and place in an ice-cream maker and churn according to the manufacturer's directions.

To make the raspberry sauce, mix the raspberry purée and sugar syrup to taste and set aside.

Whip the mascarpone, sour cream, lemon zest and a little icing sugar together to form a thickened cream. Spoon into the tart cases to fill two-thirds of each case. Place the raspberries on the cream to cover the surface. Drizzle a little sauce over the raspberries and sprinkle with icing sugar. Serve with the raspberry sorbet.

Mascarpone pannacotta
with poached rhubarb

Another great marriage of tastes—rhubarb and pannacotta were made for each other. A very light melt-in-the-mouth pannacotta which still retains a certain firmness. The method for poaching rhubarb is a great technique as the gentle cooking allows it to retain its shape. It can all be made the day before.

Ingredients

Pannacotta

2 teaspoons powdered gelatine

2 tablespoons water

⅓ cup vanilla caster sugar

1¼ cups sour cream

⅔ cup mascarpone

1 vanilla bean, split lengthwise

1½ tablespoons lemon juice

1¼ cups thickened cream, whipped

Rhubarb

450 g rhubarb, leaves removed

1½ cups water

2 tablespoons grenadine syrup

⅔ cup sugar

Serves 10

To make the pannacotta, sprinkle the gelatine over the water in a small bowl and leave to dissolve. Whisk together the sugar, sour cream and mascarpone in a large stainless steel bowl. Split the vanilla bean lengthwise and scrape out the seeds. Add the seeds and bean to the mascarpone bowl and place it over a saucepan of simmering water. When the sour cream mixture is warm, add the dissolved gelatine and mix well. Continue heating the sour cream mixture, stirring continuously with a wooden spoon until the mixture reaches 62°C. Stir in the lemon juice, then strain through a fine sieve into a clean bowl. Set the bowl over iced water and keep stirring. Let the mixture begin to thicken a little, whisk gently and fold in the whipped cream. Pour the mixture into ramekins and refrigerate for 3–4 hours.

To cook the rhubarb, bring a large saucepan of water to a simmer. Meanwhile, peel the rhubarb to remove any rough edges and cut the stalks on the bias
Continued overleaf

LEFT: Mascarpone pannacotta with poached rhubarb

RIGHT: Caramelised figs, yellowbox honey ice-cream and orange caramel sauce (recipe overleaf)

into lengths. Pack the rhubarb in a large resealable freezerbag. Add the water, grenadine syrup and sugar, mix and close the bag securely. Put the bag into simmering water and poach the fruit for 20 minutes, never allowing the water to boil. Carefully lift the bag out of the water and keeping the bag sealed, press a few pieces of rhubarb between your fingers. If the rhubarb is tender it's ready. If it's not, give it a few more minutes. Transfer the bag to a rack and cool to room temperature, then chill overnight in the refrigerator.

To serve, remove the rhubarb from its bag and pour into a bowl. Spoon some stalks and juices into deep serving bowls. Unmould the pannacottas and place on top of the rhubarb. Serve with a crisp wafer or add some slices of strawberries if desired.

Passionfruit sorbet

Passionfruit makes a fresh-tasting sorbet because its natural acidity is a balance for the essential sugar required to make a smooth sorbet.

Ingredients

About 20 passionfruit

½ **cup water**

1½ **cups sugar syrup (page 140)**

Serves 10

To prepare the sorbet, halve the passionfruit, scoop out the flesh and place in the bowl of a food processor. Using the pulse button, blend the purée just enough to loosen the seeds from the pulp and juices. Place the purée in a sieve over a bowl and strain all the juices, pushing down hard on the pulp to ensure as much juice as possible is extracted. You need ¾ cup of juice.

Place the passionfruit juice, water and sugar syrup in a bowl and whisk together to blend. Churn the sorbet in an ice-cream maker according to the manufacturer's instructions, remove and keep frozen until needed.

Caramelised figs,

yellowbox honey ice-cream and
orange caramel sauce

I'm a great fan of the 'warmed fruit with ice-cream' dessert—the contrast of temperatures offers the best of blends. Figs begin appearing in late summer and blend beautifully with the yellowbox honey. The very versatile orange caramel sauce rounds it all out nicely.

Ingredients

Honey ice-cream

2 cups milk

½ cup yellowbox honey

6 egg yolks

½ cup caster sugar

2 cups cream

Orange caramel sauce

½ cup orange zest

¼ cup caster sugar

⅘ cup fresh orange juice, strained

1 tablespoon fresh lemon juice, strained

1 tablespoon cornflour

1 tablespoon Grand Marnier

8 fresh figs

2 tablespoons caster sugar

8 Pistachio wafers (page 139)

24 raspberries or strawberries

Serves 8

YELLOWBOX HONEY
Yellowbox honey has a mellow rounded flavour. A rich honey, like ironbark, is too strong for this ice-cream.

To make the honey ice-cream, put the milk and honey in a saucepan and slowly bring to the boil over a low heat, stirring, to dissolve the honey. Place the egg yolks and sugar in a bowl and whisk until the mixture whitens. Pour a little of the honey mixture over the yolks, whisk to blend, and then stir this mixture back into the original saucepan.

To make a crème anglaise, place the saucepan over a low heat and stir until the custard is 85°C or coats the back of the stirringspoon. Strain into a bowl through a fine sieve, add the cream and cool over a bowl of ice. When chilled, churn in an ice-cream maker according to the manufacturer's directions. When frozen, mould the ice-cream into deep egg rings (2.5 cm deep x 7.5 cm diameter) and freeze again until needed.

To prepare the orange caramel sauce, place the orange zest in a small saucepan, cover with water and bring to the boil. Simmer for 4 minutes, strain, keeping 1½ tablespoons of the poaching liquid. Place the zest and poaching liquid in another small saucepan with the sugar and cook over a medium heat to caramelise; that is, dissolve the sugar and boil until the liquid reaches a rich golden brown. Carefully, in case it bubbles up, add the orange and lemon juices to the saucepan, return to a boil and stir until the caramel dissolves. Mix the cornflour with the Grand Marnier, whisk it into the hot sauce and boil for 1–2 minutes. Remove from the heat and cool. Strain the sauce through a fine sieve and keep aside until needed.

To caramelise the figs, cut the figs into quarters, dip the cut sides into the sugar and caramelise with a blowtorch or under a hot grill.

To serve, unmould the ice-cream and place in the centre of bowls or plates. Top with a round pistachio wafer made about the same size as the ice-cream mould and spoon sauce around the ice-cream. Top with the warm figs and raspberries.

Bittersweet chocolate framboise fondant

A beautifully smooth, rich, yet meltingly delicious chocolate dessert using that classic taste combination—raspberries paired with chocolate. If you belong to the camp which believes chocolate and raspberries don't enhance each other—this fondant may help to convince you otherwise. The measurements of ingredients in this recipe are critical so they must be weighed.

Ingredients

Chocolate sheet sponge

25 g cocoa powder

25 g flour

25 g potato flour

125 g egg yolks

65 g caster sugar + 60 g caster sugar

125 g eggwhites

55 g melted butter

Chocolate fondant

1½ (5 g) sheets gelatine leaves

1 cup (250 ml) milk

1 cup (250 ml) cream

8 egg yolks

½ cup (100 g) caster sugar

400 g bittersweet chocolate, chopped

5 tablespoons (100 ml) Raspberry purée (page 113), strained

1½ tablespoons (30 ml) framboise eau-de-vie

30 raspberries

Chocolate icing (optional)

50 g bittersweet chocolate

2½ tablespoons (50 ml) cream

Serves 10

RIGHT: Bittersweet chocolate framboise fondant

To make the chocolate sheet sponge, line a buttered flat sponge tray with baking paper and preheat the oven to 220°C. Sift the cocoa powder, flour and potato flour together in a bowl. In another bowl, whisk the egg yolks and 65 g caster sugar together until the mixture is white and forms a ribbon when dropped from the whisk back into the bowl. In a clean, dry, stainless steel bowl whisk the eggwhites to soft peaks and then gradually add the remaining 60 g of caster sugar while whisking. Continue until the whites are quite stiff. Fold half the egg-white mixture into the egg yolk mixture, sift over the cocoa flour mixture and fold in with the remaining stiffened whites. Finally fold in the melted butter.

Distribute the batter evenly over the prepared baking tray with a metal spatula. Bake for 8–10 minutes in the preheated oven. The sponge should show a little resistance when touched with your finger and show signs of coming away from the edge of the tray when ready. Remove from the oven and slip the sponge from the tray onto a wire rack to cool.

Remove the baking paper and cut the sponge into portions, or store in an airtight container. The sponge also freezes very well.

To make the fondant, first prepare the moulds. Using round rings, 65 cm diameter x 40 mm high, cut out chocolate sponge rounds. Place a sponge at the base of each ring mould and place on a flat tray lined with greaseproof or baking paper.

Soak the gelatine leaves in water for 5 minutes. Place the milk and cream in a saucepan over a medium heat and bring almost to the boil. Meanwhile, whisk the egg yolks and sugar together in a bowl to whiten and thicken. Pour the hot cream-milk *Continued overleaf*

mixture onto the egg yolks and whisk to blend. Pour back into the saucepan and stir over a low heat to make a crème anglaise (custard) until it is 85°C or until the back of the stirringspoon remains well coated. Remove from the heat, add the chocolate and whisk in to melt. Squeeze out the gelatine leaves and whisk into the warm chocolate mixture to dissolve. Mix the raspberry purée with the eau-de-vie and then whisk into the chocolate mixture. Place the chocolate bowl over another bowl of iced water and whisk continuously until the mixture begins to thicken a little and take on some body— it will form a ribbon when dropped from the whisk back into the bowl.

Place 3 raspberries on top of the sponge in each ring and pour in enough chocolate mixture to fill the rings. Give the tray a slight tap on the bench to settle each mould and place the chocolates in the refrigerator to set overnight.

When ready to serve the fondants, take them from the refrigerator, remove the metal rings and place them in the centre of each plate. The fondants can be served with your favourite chocolate sorbet or Honey ice-cream (page 117), and can be topped with chocolate icing if desired.

To make the chocolate icing, place the chocolate in a small stainless steel bowl. Place the cream in a small saucepan and nearly bring to the boil, then pour it over the chocolate. Swirl the bowl to help melt the chocolate, but don't stir it. Leave the icing to cool for 10 minutes. Remove the set fondants from the refrigerator and place a spoonful of icing on top of one fondant. Tip the mould so the icing runs to the edges and coats the top evenly. Repeat with the remaining fondants. Return to the refrigerator to set.

Moist orange-syrup cake

I like to bake this delicious orange cake in a shallow tart case rather than a cake tin. It looks better and the syrup penetrates the cake more easily.

Ingredients

225 g unsalted butter + extra

1¼ cups (165 g) flour + extra

2½ teaspoons (11 g) baking powder

1¾ cups (225 g) icing sugar, sifted or sieved

3 eggs

⅖ cup (100 ml) orange juice, strained

3 oranges, zested

Orange syrup

⅖ cup (100 ml) orange juice, strained

1 cup + 2½ tablespoons (150 g) icing sugar, sieved

1 tablespoon kirsh or grand marnier

1 cup whipped cream

Serves 8–10

To prepare the cake, butter a 28 cm diameter tart case, preferably Teflon. Line the bottom of the case with baking paper. Butter the paper and then sprinkle with some extra flour. Invert to remove any excess flour and set aside. Preheat the oven to 200°C.

Sieve the flour and baking powder together and set aside. Place the sieved icing sugar in an electric mixer bowl with the paddle attachment. Melt 225 g of unsalted butter over a very-low heat, watching carefully so it just melts and doesn't separate. Immediately pour it over the icing sugar in the bowl and whisk on medium-high speed. The mixture will separate slightly but keep whisking until it becomes creamy. Add the eggs one at a time, incorporating each egg before adding another. Pour in the orange juice slowly and continue to blend until it is all absorbed. Lower the speed and add the flour, baking powder mixture and the orange zest and mix to blend.

To cook the cake, pour the mixture into the prepared tart case and bake in the preheated oven for 10 minutes. Lower the temperature to 175°C and continue baking for 15–20 minutes. Test with a toothpick—when it comes out clean the cake is ready. The cake should be golden brown and coming away from the sides slightly. Remove from the oven, place on a wire cake rack and cool in the case. Unmould the cake onto a flat platter while it is still slightly warm and prepare the orange syrup.

To make the orange syrup, place the orange juice and icing sugar in a saucepan over medium heat and whisk to dissolve the icing sugar. Add the liqueur. Remove from the heat and keep brushing the syrup over the cake until all the syrup is absorbed.

To serve, slice the cake and serve with the whipped cream. A salad of strawberries and orange segments would also accompany the cake nicely.

Coconut dacquoise

and coconut ice-cream with mango, and lime sauce

A natural combination of summer dessert flavours. A dacquoise is a light, crisp meringue softened with almonds or coconut.

Ingredients

Coconut ice cream

2¼ cups desiccated coconut

4½ cups milk

12 egg yolks

1¾ cups sugar

2 cups cream

2½ tablespoons coconut liqueur (optional)

Coconut dacquoise

½ cup icing sugar

2 tablespoons almond meal

1 cup desiccated coconut

150 ml eggwhites

Pinch cream of tartar

2 tablespoons caster sugar

8 limes

¾ cup of sugar

1⅕ cups water

5 mangoes, ripe

¼ cup green pistachios, chopped

Serves 10

LEFT: Coconut dacquoise and ice-cream with mango, and lime sauce

To make the coconut ice-cream, place the coconut in a stainless steel saucepan and cover with the milk. Let it rest for 10 minutes. Place the milk and coconut over a medium heat and bring to a near boil, stirring occasionally. Remove from the heat and leave to infuse for 5 minutes. Meanwhile, with a whisk or hand-held electric beater, cream the egg yolks and sugar together in a bowl until white and thick. Strain the coconut-infused milk through a large chinois or fine sieve, into a clean bowl, pressing down on the coconut with a wooden mushroom or potato masher to extract all the milk. There should be 1 litre of milk. Strain the milk through a fine chinois into the original saucepan which has been cleaned, and return to a near boil over a low heat. Pour the hot milk over the egg yolk mixture, blend well and return to a medium heat. Using a wooden spoon, continually stir the custard until it begins to thicken and coats the back of the spoon. Strain into a bowl, add the cream and cool over a bowl of ice. When cold, add the coconut liqueur and churn in an ice-cream maker according to the manufacturer's directions. When frozen, mould the ice-cream into 10 deep egg rings and freeze.

To make the coconut dacquoise, blend the icing sugar, almond meal and desiccated coconut in a food processor until they are blended well. Preheat the oven to 180°C. Line a baking tray with baking paper the same size as the tray. Whisk the eggwhites in a bowl with a pinch of cream of tartar until it is beginning to foam and form soft peaks. Gradually add the caster sugar and continue to beat to form a firm snow-like texture. Fold in the dry coconut mixture carefully, but you must work quickly as the meringue has a large amount of sugar folded in at the end of the mixture and will begin to weep unless you are fast. Pour the meringue into a piping bag and pipe small discs onto the baking paper. Pipe your discs slightly smaller than the diameter of your ice-cream moulds as the dacquoise will spread a little during baking. Bake in the preheated oven for 15–25 minutes depending on size. The dacquoise should be *Continued overleaf* light-brown but will feel slightly soft. They harden on contact with air as they cool. Remove the paper from underneath the dacquoise; a little water will help. Leave to cool on racks and store in an airtight container until needed, placing baking paper between the layers.

To make the lime sauce, first grate the zest from the limes. Place the sugar, zest and 300 ml water in a saucepan. Bring to the boil and simmer for 30 minutes. Remove from the heat and leave to infuse for 1 hour. Squeeze the juice from 4 of the limes, strain and add to the syrup. Strain the sauce through a fine sieve into a clean container and keep refrigerated.

To prepare the mangoes, peel, then slice them into halves on either side of the stone. Slice the mango thinly into lengthwise strips and form a circle by fanning it between your palms and cupping it in your hands. Lift each mango circle onto a tray, cover with cling-wrap and place in the refrigerator for 15 minutes to allow the mango slices to stick to one another.

To complete the dish, place a dacquoise in the centre of the dessert bowls. Unmould the ice-cream ring and place one on each dacquoise. Top with the fanned mango circle and pour the lime sauce over and around the ice-cream. Sprinkle with a few pistachios and serve.

Coconut and mango financiers

A delicious buttery and coconut-textured cake.

FINANCIERS

Originally financiers were baked in small tins resembling gold bouillon— hence the name. They are a great after-dinner nibble to serve with coffee if you make small financiers in petit four moulds. These cakes can also be a dessert course baked in larger moulds and served with fresh fruit and ice-cream. Other fruit tastes good inside these cakes too—try using blueberries, banana, raspberries, plums and nectarines.

Ingredients

250 g unsalted butter

¾ cup (65 g) dessicated coconut

¾ cup (65 g) ground white almonds

1 cup (125 g) flour

2 cups (250 g) icing sugar

1 teaspoon baking powder

Zest 1 lemon

8 eggwhites

1–2 mangoes, cubed

Makes 20 petits fours or 10 small cakes

To prepare the financiers, place the butter in a saucepan and melt over a low heat. Purée the coconut and almonds in a food processor until they are finely blended. Combine the flour, icing sugar, baking powder, zest, almonds and coconut mix in a large bowl. Add half the eggwhites and stir with a wooden spoon until combined. Repeat with the remaining eggwhites. Lightly mix in the warm melted butter and combine.

To cook the financiers, preheat the oven to 190°C. Butter the moulds (preferably Teflon) well, or use small muffin tins or small tart cases and fill each mould ¾ full. Push a piece of mango into the centre of each financier mould. Bake in the preheated oven until a nice pale-gold colour on top. The small financiers will take about 15 minutes and larger moulds about 30 minutes. Test with a toothpick in the centre of a cake—if it comes out dry they are ready. When cooked, turn out of the moulds and cool on a rack. There will be some mixture left over but it will keep refrigerated for 4–5 days.

Strawberry shortcakes

Strawberry shortcakes are a great dessert as long as you don't make them too large. Let the strawberries and the sauces shine and the shortcake act as a backdrop. Tossing the strawberries just before you serve them in lemon or orange juice and icing sugar, heightens their flavour.

Ingredients

Shortcakes

2⅓ cups (300 g) flour

1½ teaspoons sea salt

1 tablespoon baking powder

2 tablespoons sugar

105 g unsalted butter, chilled, cut into small dice

¾ cup cream + extra

1 tablespoon caster sugar

Strawberry sauce

¾ cup strawberries

2 tablespoons caster sugar

½ teaspoon lemon juice

1⅓ cup Crème anglaise (page 140)

2 cups strawberries

1 tablespoon icing sugar + extra

1 tablespoon lemon juice

Serves 8

To prepare the shortcakes, preheat the oven to 190°C. Mix the flour, salt, baking powder and sugar together in a large bowl. Rub the diced butter into the flour base with your hands until the mixture resembles coarse breadcrumbs. Continue to mix and slowly add the cream until the dough comes together. Turn the dough out onto a floured bench and using the heel of your palm, give the dough a final knead to combine lightly.

To cook the shortcakes, lightly flour the bench and using a rolling pin, roll the dough out gently until 2 cm thick. Cut out the shortcakes with a 55 mm diameter pastry cutter. Place the shortcakes on a flat tray lined with baking paper. Brush the top of each shortcake with a little cream and sprinkle each with sugar. Bake the shortcakes in the preheated oven for 7 minutes, turn the tray and bake for another 7 minutes. The shortcakes should be lightly browned and the dough set, but not hard. They will still be quite moist in the centre. Remove the shortcakes from the oven and cool on a rack.

To make the strawberry sauce, remove any stems from the strawberries and place in a blender bowl. Add the caster sugar and purée on high speed until completely blended. Remove from the blender and pass through a fine sieve into another bowl. Add lemon juice to taste.

To serve the shortcakes, slice them in half horizontally and place the bottom of each shortcake in the centre of the plates. Spoon 2 tablespoons of crème anglaise around each shortcake. Cut the strawberries into quarters or sixths if they are large and place in a bowl. Add the icing sugar and lemon juice to heighten the flavour of the strawberries and toss gently but thoroughly to macerate. Spoon an equal amount of strawberries between the plates on top of the shortcake bases. Spoon some strawberry sauce over and around the strawberries in a nice circular pattern. Dust each shortcake top with icing sugar and place on top of the strawberries and sauces and serve. An alternative is to serve a scoop of rich vanilla ice-cream, strawberry ice-cream or strawberry sorbet—all complement this dish perfectly.

Back to basics

The following recipes and techniques are referred to throughout the book. These basics are the foundation and highlight of many of my dishes.

Good stock is an important base for good sauces and soups. A large heavy-based stockpot is a good investment for the domestic kitchen. It enables you to make a large quantity of stock and store the extra in the freezer for future use. Some of the sauces that accompany my meat and poultry dishes require stock. By reducing stock with a few specific ingredients you are concentrating the flavours that give elusive depth to many dishes. Some of the sauces, such as the Almond tarator, Tomato sauce, Caper and vegetable salsa and the Flavoured oils, are infinitely adaptable to recipes in different chapters. Others such as the Vinaigrettes are simply indispensable. These are used repeatedly throughout the book and used to add flavour to favourites such as the Salad of herbs and the Roasted red capsicums.

Certain basics, like the Polenta, which I urge you to make, and the Ravioli pasta, will expand your understanding of these basics and lead you to many hours of enjoyment in the kitchen. Others, such as the Sugar syrup and Crème anglaise, are used daily in the restaurant kitchen and many sorbets, ice-creams, bavarois, parfaits and sauces all begin with these two fundamentals.

Correct seasoning is possibly the most important basic technique any cook can learn. Sometimes I don't season the main ingredient, such as salmon, before cooking because essential moisture would be drawn out. Instead, the fish will be sprinkled with sea salt just before serving. In most cases I recommend you to season lightly but often, and taste as you go. A dish such as the Grilled octopus and prawns on kipfler potatoes with tomato herb vinaigrette requires the correct seasoning of all its components. The Potato salad will absorb quite a lot of salt before you really get the balance right but when you have it will come alive. The tomatoes should not be seasoned until they are mixed with the seasoned vinaigrette or the salt will extract too much liquid and break down the flavour of the vinaigrette. The prawns and octopus are seasoned just before grilling. The beans, which have been cooked in salty water, will require further seasoning just before being placed on the potatoes. Seasoning this way you create layers of heightened flavour and the dish tastes well seasoned.

RIGHT: Almond tarator sauce (recipe overleaf)

Almond tarator sauce

A Turkish sauce traditionally served with cooked vegetable salads.

Ingredients

½ **loaf Italian-style bread, crust removed**

1 **cup finely ground white almonds or walnuts**

2 **garlic cloves, peeled and smashed**

5 **tablespoons water**

4 **tablespoons fresh lemon juice**

3 **tablespoons extra-virgin olive oil**

3 **tablespoons water**

Sea salt and freshly ground black pepper

Makes about 2 cups

To make the almond tarator sauce, dip the bread in water to saturate, remove and squeeze dry. You should have ⅔ cup of bread. Place the ground almond in a food processor with the garlic and blend with the 5 tablespoons of water to form a smooth paste. Add the bread and lemon juice and blend again to a smooth texture. Leave the machine turned on and add the extra-virgin olive oil in a thin stream followed by the 3 tablespoons of water. Season with salt and pepper and check the lemon. The sauce may need more water whisked in before serving. Keeps 4–5 days, refrigerated.

Clarified butter

Clarified butter has a much higher burning point than butter because all the solids have been extracted. It can be stored indefinitely.

Ingredients

500 g unsalted butter

Makes 1 ¾ cups

To clarify the butter, place it in a small stainless steel container or a saucepan. Make a bain-marie by placing the saucepan in a baking tray which is half-filled with water. Put over a very low heat and leave the butter to clarify for about 20–30 minutes. Ladle off any scum as it forms on the surface. When the butter has clarified, ladle it out into a container, being careful not to disturb the solids at the bottom. Refrigerate covered, when cool.

Paprika oil

A beautifully coloured infused oil. Combine with strained lemon juice to make a vinaigrette and use with dishes where paprika is used as a spice.

Ingredients

1 ½ **tablespoons sweet paprika**

1 **cup extra-virgin olive oil**

Makes 1 cup

Place the paprika in a stainless steel saucepan and slowly whisk in the oil. When well mixed, warm it over a low heat. Remove and leave to cool. Strain through a very fine sieve twice. Stores for up to 2 weeks, refrigerated.

Red-wine vinaigrette

I like to keep my basic vinaigrette simple using good quality ingredients. The acidity balance is the other important aspect—don't make it too acidic.

Ingredients

1 cup extra-virgin olive oil

2½ tablespoons red-wine vinegar

Salt and freshly ground black pepper

Makes 1¼ cups

Whisk the ingredients and season to taste. For sherry vinaigrette, substitute sherry vinegar for the red wine. Keeps for 3 days, refrigerated.

Lemon vinaigrette

Lemon vinaigrette is used as a basic dressing throughout the book.

Ingredients

2½ tablespoons fresh lemon juice, strained

1 cup extra-virgin olive oil

Sea salt and freshly ground black pepper

Makes 1¼ cups

To prepare the lemon vinaigrette, place the lemon juice in a stainless steel bowl and gradually whisk in the olive oil. Season with salt and pepper. Fresh lemon juice has a short life (1 day only) so make as needed. Keeps for 3 days, refrigerated.

Anchovy and tarragon butter

Enjoy this savoury butter with grilled steak, lamb or chicken and even seafood. It is very handy for adding flavour to quickly prepared grills.

Ingredients

2 tablespoons finely chopped golden shallots

5 tablespoons white wine

3 teaspoons chopped fresh tarragon leaves

8 anchovy fillets

½ teaspoon minced garlic

Sea salt and freshly ground black pepper

1 tablespoon mustard

1 tablespoon lemon juice

250 g unsalted butter, softened

2 tablespoons chopped fresh flat-leaf parsley

Serves 10–15

To prepare the anchovy butter, place the shallots, wine and tarragon in a small saucepan and reduce over a medium heat to a moist purée. Place the shallot reduction into the bowl of a food processor and add the anchovy fillets, garlic, salt, pepper and mustard and blend. Add the lemon juice and continue blending. Then add the butter and blend until you achieve a smooth paste. Add the chopped parsley and blend. Roll into a log shape and wrap in cling-film. Refrigerate if not using immediately and soften before use—just cut off a few slices per serve. Keeps for up to 2 weeks, refrigerated.

Chicken stock

An indispensable stock. You need some meaty chicken parts (I like the wings), to produce a rich chicken stock.

Ingredients

2 kg chicken bones, chopped

2 kg chicken wings, chopped

Water

1 onion, peeled, halved

1 carrot, peeled, halved

1 stalk celery

3 cm piece ginger, sliced in half

4 parsley stalks

1 bay leaf

3 sprigs fresh thyme

Makes about 3 litres

LEFT: A good chicken stock is an important element of Summer pea and zucchini risotto (recipe page 53)

To prepare the stock, place the bones and wings in a large stainless steel stockpot, cover the bones with water by 10 cm, and bring to the boil. Reduce the heat and skim off any scum which surfaces. Simmer on a low heat and add the remaining ingredients. Cook for 3–4 hours until the stock tastes rich and has taken on a little golden colour. Strain through a fine sieve into a container and cool. When cool, refrigerate until the fats on top solidify and can be easily removed. The stock is now ready to be used as needed or frozen. It can be kept for up to 1 week refrigerated with the fat sealing the top. Keeps for 3 months in the freezer.

Fish stock

Ask for the fresh bones of non-oily white fish and slice the vegetables finely as fish stock doesn't cook for long. Use a stainless steel stockpot for fish stock.

Ingredients

3 kg fishbones

1 onion, finely sliced

1 leek, finely sliced

1 stalk celery, finely sliced

1 garlic clove, sliced in half

2 tablespoons olive oil

½ cup white wine

5 fresh parsley springs or stalks

½ teaspoon peppercorns

4 litres water

Makes about 3 litres

To prepare the fish stock, thoroughly rinse the fishbones in plenty of water so that no blood remains and the water runs clear. Drain well. Place the onions, leeks, celery and garlic with the olive oil in a stainless steel stockpot and sweat over a low heat for 4 minutes. Add the fishbones, white wine, parsley and peppercorns and reduce over a low heat to almost nothing. Add the water to just cover the ingredients and bring to the boil slowly. Skim the surface of any scum as it develops. Bringing the stock to the boil slowly will produce a clearer stock. Once the stock boils, reduce the heat and simmer for 20 minutes. Remove from the heat and allow the stock to settle for 15 minutes. Carefully ladle the stock through a sieve lined with muslin, trying not to disturb the stock contents too much. Cool and refrigerate for up to 2 days, or freeze until needed (up to 3 months).

Veal stock

An essential ingredient in good meat braises and the base of many sauces.

Ingredients

2 kg veal bones

2 kg beef bones

500 g beef shin meat

2 carrots, thinly sliced

1 stalk celery, halved

2 onions, halved

Bouquet garni (thyme, parsley, bay leaves, peppercorns)

⅓ cup tomato paste

Water

Makes about 5 litres

LONG-SIMMERING STOCKS Make these stocks over the weekend and enjoy the pleasant aromas in your home. To save time and effort, buy a large stockpot, 16–20 litres, so you can make large quantities of stock to freeze for future use.

To make the stock, preheat the oven to 200°C. Place the veal and beef bones with the shin on a roasting tray and brown in the preheated oven for about 40 minutes taking care not to burn the bones. Prepare the carrots, celery and onions and add to the browning bones for the last 10 minutes.

Remove the bones, meat and vegetables and place in a large stockpot. Add the bouquet garni and tomato paste and cover the ingredients with cold water by 15 cm. Bring to the boil, reduce the heat and simmer slowly for at least 6 hours. During this time, skim any collected scum or oil from the surface regularly.

Strain the stock through a fine strainer into a container and cool. When cool, refrigerate until the fats on top turn solid and can be easily removed. The stock is now ready to be reboiled and used for braising or reduced to obtain a rich concentrated stock. It will store in the refrigerator for up to a week with the fat as a seal or it will freeze successfully for up to 3 months.

Reduced veal stock sauce

A rich flavourful base sauce used extensively to complement meat dishes. The flavours may vary to suit individual dishes by adding different, but harmonising, herbs and spices.

Ingredients

6 golden shallots or 1 onion

2 tablespoons white-wine vinegar

1 cup white wine

2 cups Veal stock (as above)

3 fresh thyme sprigs

Makes 1½ cups

To make the sauce, peel and finely chop the shallots. Place the shallots and the vinegar in a stainless steel saucepan over a medium-high heat and reduce to almost nothing. Add the white wine and reduce by half. Add the veal stock and thyme and bring to the boil. Lower the heat and simmer until the sauce has reduced by half and has a rich flavour. Remove from the heat, strain through a fine sieve and use immediately, or cool and refrigerate for 3 days or freeze for up to 3 months.

Polenta

This enlightened method of cooking polenta is for those who hate the tedium of stirring for 30–40 minutes. It even produces a better and smoother result.

Ingredients

250 g polenta

2 teaspoons sea salt

5 cups water

65 g unsalted butter

½ cup grated parmesan cheese

Serves 10 or more

FRIED OR BAKED POLENTA Pour the polenta into a large 2.5 cm deep tray lined with baking paper, smooth the top with a rubber spatula and a little butter. Refrigerate to cool and harden. Cut into the required shape, dust with flour and fry in vegetable oil at 180°C for 3 minutes or until crusty and golden brown. Drain on absorbent paper towels. Keep warm in a medium-hot oven at 180°C while finishing your dish.

To cook the polenta, put a large saucepan half-filled with water over a high heat and bring to the boil. Lower the heat and leave the water to simmer. Place the polenta and salt in a large stainless steel bowl that is big enough to fit on top of the saucepan to create a double boiler. In another saucepan bring the 5 cups of water to the boil. Once boiling, pour the water onto the polenta, one third at a time, whisking vigorously. Continue with the remaining polenta until it is blended and lump-free.

Cover the polenta with a light lid or foil and secure the edges. Set the polenta over the large saucepan of simmering water, check the bowl doesn't touch the water and cook for 1½ hours, keeping the water simmering. Every 20 minutes, during the cooking, use a rubber spatula to stir the polenta, scooping down to the bottom of the bowl to stop the mixture from sticking. Replace the lid or foil each time.

After 1½ hours add the butter and grated parmesan cheese to the polenta and whisk in well to blend. Check the seasoning. The polenta should be thick, smooth, and have no suggestion of rawness in its taste.

To serve, use immediately, or keep warm over a saucepan of hot water in a warm place if using as soft polenta. Cover the polenta with buttered waxpaper and a tight-fitting lid. You will need to whisk in warm water just before you serve the polenta, because it will thicken as it rests.

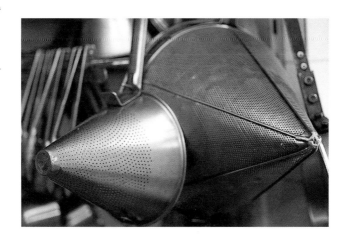

Crostini or croûtons

These crostini can never taste better than the bread used so buy good-quality French- or Italian-style breads—wood-fired breads and sourdoughs are best.

Ingredients
1 crusty bread loaf or baguette, thinly sliced

3 tablespoons extra-virgin olive oil

1 clove garlic, sliced across, optional

To prepare the crostini, preheat the grill. Place the sliced bread on the tray and place the tray on the lowest rack away from the grill, at least 30 cm. The trick is to dry the bread out toasting it at the same time. When it is golden-brown, turn the bread over and toast lightly on the second side. Remove and rub the croûton with garlic if using or just paint lightly with the olive oil. Set aside until needed.

To prepare the croûtons, brush the bread slices with oil and dry out in a preheated oven at 190°C until the croûtons are golden on both sides, about 6–8 minutes. Keeps for 1 day only.

VARIATION

To make tapenade croûtons, spread the cooked croûtons with Tapenade (page 32) just before serving.

Ravioli pasta

A very light, translucent pasta which is perfect for making ravioli and tortellini. This dough is based on Shanghai-noodle dough.

Ingredients
300 g flour

6 tablespoons boiling water

Pinch of sea salt

25 g lard

Makes 5 sheets

To make the pasta dough, place all the ingredients in the bowl of a food processor and, using the pulse button, process the pasta until it just comes together into very small balls. Remove from the bowl and place on a lightly floured bench. Knead the pasta with the heels of your palms, about 3 minutes. The pasta can be a little sticky when you begin, depending on the humidity, but keep kneading the dough to form a small ball. Place the pasta in cling-film and rest in the refrigerator for 30 minutes before continuing.

To make the pasta sheets, lay out clean tea towels to rest the sheets on then divide the dough into five equal pieces. Roll one piece out with a rolling pin until it is thin enough to go through the widest setting of your pasta machine. Roll out the other balls. Fold each piece of dough through the pasta machine on the widest setting 6 times. Then start adjusting the setting down, one notch at a time, finishing with the second last setting. Pass the pasta sheets through the second last setting twice and reserve on tea towels. Proceed according to each recipe as needed. Use fresh.

RIGHT: Crostini make the perfect accompaniment to Samfaina (recipe page 25)

Oven-dried tomatoes

Roasting tomatoes intensifies their flavour. Roast more than you need and keep them on hand—you'll find many uses for them.

Ingredients

10 ripe egg-shaped (roma) tomatoes

Sea salt and freshly ground black pepper

1 tablespoon fresh thyme leaves, chopped

4 garlic cloves, peeled, finely sliced

Extra-virgin olive oil

Makes 20 halves

Core the tomatoes, and drop them into a saucepan of boiling salted water for 10–20 seconds. Remove them with a slotted spoon and quickly refresh in a bowl of iced water. Drain, peel and cut in half lengthwise. Remove the seeds with a small spoon and place them skin side up on a wire rack over a baking sheet. Sprinkle with the salt and pepper, thyme and garlic. Roast the tomatoes in a preheated oven at 140°C for about 1½ hours or until the tomatoes have dried but still retain some of their juices. Remove from the oven, cool and keep covered with olive oil in containers in the refrigerator for up to 3 weeks. Return the tomatoes to room temperature before using, or 'flash' reheat them brushed with a little oil under a hot grill for 20 seconds.

To make oven-dried cherry tomatoes, simply cut the cherry tomatoes in half and place them, cut-side up, on a wire rack and proceed as above. Cook for 1 hour only.

Tomato sauce

I know it's been said many times before but you really do need ripe tomatoes to make a great tomato sauce. At the restaurant we use egg-shaped tomatoes and always buy them well in advance so they have time to ripen fully at room temperature before we use them.

Ingredients

¼ cup olive oil

½ small onion, finely chopped

1 kg very ripe tomatoes, peeled, seeded, chopped

3 garlic cloves, peeled, halved

4 tablespoons tomato paste

Pinch of sugar

Bouquet garni of fresh bay leaf, parsley stalks, thyme sprigs, celery stalks and peppercorns

Sea salt and freshly ground black pepper

Makes about 3 cups

Put the oil in a saucepan over a low heat, add the onion and sweat for a few minutes to soften. Add the chopped tomatoes and the remaining ingredients and cook over a medium heat for 20 minutes or more if needed. The sauce should look concentrated enough so that the pulp and juices are contained as one sauce. Remove the bouquet garni and garlic, season to taste and cool for later use. The tomato sauce can be puréed to make a sauce consistency. Add fresh herbs as needed. Store in the refrigerator in a tightly-sealed container for 1 week.

Roasted red capsicums

Handy to have on hand for summer snacks and salads. Store the capsicums in olive oil in the refrigerator for up to a week.

Ingredients

6 red capsicums

⅓ cup olive oil + extra

Makes about 1 cup

To roast the capsicums, preheat the oven to 200°C. Cut the tops off the capsicums just below the stem and tap the capsicums on the bench to remove the core and seeds. Heat the oil in a baking tray or a large frying pan over a high heat and add the capsicums. Remove the tray to the oven and roast the capsicums for about 8 minutes on the first side. The skin should have begun to blister a little without colouring. Turn the capsicums to another side and continue roasting for 5 minutes. Repeat with the remaining sides. Remove the capsicums from the oven, place on a tray and cover with cling-wrap. This helps to steam the skins and makes them easier to remove. Cool and peel the skin from the capsicums. Store in an airtight container covered in olive oil in the refrigerator for up to 1 week.

Caper and vegetable salsa

A refreshing salsa which adds a lift and textural contrast to most poached and confit fish dishes.

Ingredients

¼ cup finely diced red capsicum

¼ cup finely diced yellow capsicum

¼ cup finely diced cornichons (small gherkins)

1 tablespoon baby capers, salted, rinsed

6 anchovy fillets, finely chopped

¼ cup finely diced green olives

1 garlic clove, finely chopped

1 tablespoon sherry vinegar

5 tablespoons extra-virgin olive oil

Pinch of sea salt

Pinch of cayenne pepper

2 tablespoons finely chopped fresh parsley

1 tablespoon finely snipped fresh chives

1 tablespoon spring onions, finely diced

Makes about 1½ cups

Mix all the salsa ingredients together in a large bowl except the parsley, chives and spring onions which are added just before serving. Store in a container in the refrigerator for up to 4 days.

Salad of herbs

One of my favourite garnishes. You don't necessarily need all the herbs at one time, and in some dishes you only need a few of the lighter variety. This salad gives a real lift to many dishes and provides a freshness and variety of flavour.

Ingredients

1 tablespoon fresh coriander leaves

⅓ cup fresh flat-leaf parsley

2 teaspoons fresh tarragon leaves

⅓ cup fresh dill, picked into fronds

⅓ cup fresh chervil, picked into small bunches

1 cup curly endive, white inner-leaves only

2 tablespoons baby landcress, optional

2 tablespoons edible flower petals; marigold, nasturtium and borage are good

Makes about 10 garnishes

Pick over the herbs very carefully and detach the coriander, parsley and tarragon from their tough stems. The dill, chervil, and endive should be picked into small trays. Drop the herbs into a bowl of water to keep them fresh. Pay particular attention to the quantities of each herb as some are stronger than others and you need a balance of flavours. When the herbs have been picked in sufficient quantities, rinse lightly and drain very well in a colander or sieve. Place in a salad-spinner and spin gently because of the delicate nature of the herbs. Keep in an airtight container in the refrigerator until needed. Toss lightly with vinaigrette just before serving.

Pistachio wafers

A clean-tasting, crisp, very light wafer—ideal to serve with dessert.

Ingredients

3 eggwhites

½ cup caster sugar

4 ½ tablespoons flour

2 ½ tablespoons unsalted butter, melted

1 tablespoon green pistachios, chopped

Makes about 40

LEFT: Salad of herbs makes a perfect garnish on Crisp potato galette, grilled goat's cheese, oven-dried tomatoes and herb salad (recipe page 52)

To make the batter, place the eggwhites in a bowl and beat slightly with a spoon. Add the sugar and mix well. Then add the flour and mix in well. Add the melted butter and beat until the mixture is smooth. Refrigerate for 1–3 hours in an airtight container before cooking.

To cook the wafers, place 2 teaspoons of the batter onto a Teflon tray (which has been placed in the freezer to get very cold). Using the back of a dessertspoon, work the batter in a circular motion to spread it into a 5 cm circle. Leave some space between the wafers and continue until the sheet is full. Sprinkle the wafers with the chopped pistachios. There will be more batter than you need depending on how large the wafers are (the batter will keep refrigerated for 4–5 days). Bake in a preheated oven at 155°C until the edges are golden, about 5–7 minutes. Remove from the oven, leave to cool for 10–15 seconds and then carefully lift the wafers from the tray and lay flat on a bench to cool and harden. The shape can also be twisted before they harden into a tuile (tile) shape or desired shape. Once cooled, store in an airtight container—they keep for 3 days.

Crème anglaise

The base for many ice-creams, bavarois and sauces, crème anglaise is a rich, smooth creamy custard. Cooking the sauce to 85°C ensures it will have a velvety consistency.

Ingredients

½ **vanilla bean, split**

2 cups milk

2 tablespoons sugar

6 egg yolks

½ **cup sugar**

1 teaspoon vanilla extract

Makes about 3 cups

To prepare the custard, place the vanilla bean on a bench, split and scrape the seeds out with a teaspoon. Place the milk and sugar in a saucepan and add the vanilla seeds and bean. Bring to a near boil over a medium heat.

Meanwhile, whisk the egg yolks and the sugar in a bowl together until they have whitened and thickened. Pour the boiled milk onto the egg yolk mixture and whisk well to blend. Return the custard to the hot saucepan and put it over a low heat. Stir the custard constantly with a wooden spoon until it coats the back of the spoon and leaves a line down the spoon when you run your finger down it or until the sauce registers 85°C on a cooking thermometer. Remove from the heat and strain through a fine sieve into another clean bowl and cool. Store in an airtight container, refrigerated, for up to 4 days.

Sugar syrup

The base used in sorbets, compôtes, sauces and some ice-creams. It also keeps well for months in the refrigerator so keep some on hand.

Ingredients

4 cups water

3½ **cups sugar**

Makes about 7 cups

To make the sugar syrup, place the water in a stainless steel saucepan, add the sugar and place over a high heat. Whisk to help dissolve the sugar, and bring to a boil. Once it has boiled, remove from the heat and cool.

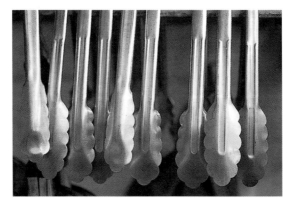

Glossary

al dente: means 'firm to the bite'—not mushy or soft, used to describe pasta, rice and some vegetables.

bain-marie: a hot water bath used to diffuse direct heat. A bowl or pan of food is placed in a shallow pan of simmering water.

blanch: vegetables are boiled for a few minutes to preserve their colour and texture, and then refreshed. Meat and offal are sometimes blanched to prepare them for subsequant cooking.

braise: food is slowly cooked in a covered pan in just enough liquid to barely cover the meat or vegetables.

butterfly: to split a prawn or quail down and almost through the centre. The two halves are then opened flat to resemble a butterfly.

clarified butter: the milk solids are removed from butter so that it will not burn over high heat.

deglaze: to blend concentrated juices and deposits from the bottom of the pan with a liquid such as wine or stock to simmer down into a sauce.

de-vein: to remove the dark, grittty vein from the back of a prawn with a sharp knife.

dry roasted: nuts and spices are roasted in a frying pan over heat without any oils or liquids.

emulsify: a mixture of one liquid with another which normally does not combine smoothly—oil and vinegar are whisked to make vinaigrette and egg yolk is whisked while oil is added drop by drop to make mayonnaise.

escalope: fish and meat are cut thinly on a slant to make a larger surface area to quickly sauté.

fold: eggwhites are gently incorporated into a base mixture so it retains its leavening power.

galette: French term for a thin, round cake or pastry. Galettes are also made with thin slices of overlapping vegetables and cooked in a pan on both sides, and sometimes on a thin, crisp pastry base.

grenadine syrup: a pink flavouring syrup made from pomegranates.

julienne: to cut into very thin strips or matchsticks using a knife or mandoline.

macerate: generally used to describe placing fruit in sugar and spirit to soften and give it more flavour.

mandoline: a sharp-bladed utensil for cutting firm vegetables into fine, even slices and julienne.

minced garlic: garlic cloves are peeled and chopped very finely.

shallots, green: long, thin straight onions that have a white end with roots and a green top.

shallots, golden: small, white onion-shaped bulb with brown outer skin.

spring onions: long thin green onions with a small, white, round bulb at the root end.

refresh: vegetables are plunged into iced water until completey cold after being blanched.

shaved: vegetables or cheese sliced extremely finely using a vegetable peeler or mandoline.

simmer: to maintain a gentle bubbling action after boiling by lowering the heat.

skim: to lift and discard any unwanted foam, fat or scum from the surface of stock, sauce and soup.

sweat: a technique to cook vegetables in a small amount of fat over low heat until tender and without browning.

silverskin: the bluish, tough and flat, thin sheet of connective tissue surrounding any long voluntary muscle such as lamb loin and beef fillet.

wooden mushroom: a wooden tool shaped like a wide-bottomed pestle used to push food through sieves and strainers.

tomato petals: the outer membrane of tomato flesh after a tomato has been skinned, quartered, seeded and inside pulp removed.

zest: the thin brightly coloured outer part of the rind of citrus fruits, removed with a vegetable peeler, paring knife or citrus zester.

Index

Page numbers in italics indicate illustrations